THE
PRE-FLOOD
WORLD

3000 Year Timeline to the Great Flood

CHRONICON
Part One

by

Jason M. Breshears

THE BOOK TREE
San Diego, California

ISBN 978-1-58509-160-7

Front cover image comes from a lower portion of a German copper engraving from 1678 entitled Theosophische Darstellung zur Alchemie. It is translated into English as Theosophical Presentation on Alchemy. The ancient Phoenix symbol used here was adopted into alchemy due to its recurring, transformative ability to end life — and then begin it anew.

Artificial Intelligence (AI) was not used in compiling this book, This work came from legitimate, trusted source books that took years of research to compile.

Published by
The Book Tree
San Diego, California

Contents

CHRONICON

Foreword

After 19 years data-mining over 1350 historical books, chronographic texts and reference works it has been positively determined that the events of world history are not random occurrences but fit within a series of interfacing timelines that are so perfect as to defy nature. This end product of immense research concludes affirmatively that historical events as recorded chronologically in human history are actually PROGRAMMED subroutines that converge flawlessly at key nodal interfaces in a vast, yet perfect, SIMULATION of historical events – events connected to our present awareness with such precision that a casual scrutiny of the simulation's historical protocols easily provides us EXACT future dates of when to expect similar events as had been recorded at the nodal interfaces.

Conclusion – the human experience is within the confines of a programmed simulation... the Universe is nothing more than an algorithm. It is further concluded that because Something manufactured this vast, false existence then what this false existence imprisons, *humans*, must be much more than what they suppose themselves to be. Humankind must be so immensely powerful that it was only by the deceit of a False Reality that they were subdued. Lastly, EVERY timeline connected throughout this simulated history exhibits evidence that a collapse of the simulation is planned. One after another, these false historical subroutines will collapse, with the final one ending the simulated existence at the time marked in our modern calendar at 2106 CE. Major *"reality-collapses"* will first occur in May 2040, November 2046, in 2052, and in 2070, however, the phenomena produced from the ending of these subroutines will have dual effects on human consciousness. Humans moored to the simulated false world will suffer cataclysmic episodes, ruining their civilizations, and humans who are enlightened will experience heightened awareness as the simulated deceits imprisoning them grow weaker with the collapse of each false holography.

This is the central premise to the archives of posts and books found on www.archaix.com. Come have a look, and learn what others are afraid to know.

The need for *Chronicon* is great. The world today is filled with books about global antiquities and extraterrestrial theory packed with disinformation serving only to confuse and detract from the truth. Much of the misinformation is deliberate.

The KT Boundary, Chixilub crater event, which purportedly killed off the dinosaurs 65 million years ago, was before the mass death of the megafauna (large extinct animals like wooly mammoths, giant sloths, dire wolves, etc.).

"You may indeed learn the very time when the foundation of the world was laid. If you return from this present time to former ages, you may endeavor studiously to determine the day of the world's origin. Hence, you will find when time began." –Basil the Great, in *Hexaemeron*, cited in Preface to *Ussher's Annals*.

The observations of long-forgotten sciences reappear in the world as prophecies.

Jason M. Breshears

Introduction

"...108, 216, 432, 864 and 1296 are standard measurements utilized in the construction of other megaliths throughout the globe and point to a common, worldwide organization of builders."[1]
These numbers belong to the Golden Proportion, or Phi, represented by the Fibonacci Series, defining the parameters of our collective space-time geometry, the <u>timelines</u> of human existence.

Phi, as demonstrated by the Fibonacci spiral, is a sequence of proportions, which can be found determining certain growing patters in nature.[2] This geometry is easily seen in seashells, the petal arrangement in flowers, folds of leaves and spirals of vast galaxies.

Peter Tompkins wrote, *"Phi is the symbol of generation, of procreation, or growth in all directions... It is a symbol to which all of nature subscribes, from mollusks to giant redwoods, from the structure of bones to the ages in growth in man."*[3]

For we need to understand the past five thousand years in order to master the next hundred years." C.W. Ceram, cited in *Breaking the Godspell* p. 17.

1. Return of the Serpents of Wisdom p. 87, cited from Mysteries of the Mexican Pyramids – Peter Tompkins, (1976, Harper and Row, New York); 2. Return of the Serpents of Wisdom p. 330; 3. The Magic of Obelisks, (1981, Harper & Row, New York).

20986-3895 BCE

20986 BCE (-17091 AM): 23091 Before Armageddon/ 18747 Before Flood

According to the modern scientific model, this is when light traveling from the Galactic Core at 186,000 miles per second began moving toward us to be viewed through telescopes in the year 2016 CE when the 1st draft of *Chronicon* was finished, a trip of 23,000 years.[1] A totally ridiculous notion.

1. *Earth Under Fire p. 55.*

9500 BCE (-5605 AM): 11605 Before Armageddon/ 7261 Before Flood

A plethora of modern books all borrowing from one another claim this is the approximate date for the destruction of Atlantis as told to Solon by Egyptian priests – a ridiculous dating easily proven wrong from the critical and chronological writings of Plato's critics and other works.

7819 BCE (-3924 AM): 9924 Before Armageddon/ 5580 Before Flood

A supernova occurred producing Cassiopeia A, which, being 9500 light-years away, was not visible until sighted by western astronomers in 1680 CE.[1] Again, total theory premised upon a stack of hypothetical beliefs.

1. *Earth Under Fire, p. 299.*

5531 BCE (-1636 AM): 7636 Before Armageddon/ 3292 Before Flood

A supernova occurred forming the Crab Nebula Remnant, which, being 6585 light years away, was first seen by Chinese astronomers in 1054 CE.[1] Again, there is no scientific way for we human mice to prove that the fantastically-detailed vault of lights we call the sky is anything more than a holographic projection.

"...the iridium layer associated with the disappearance of the dinosaurs came from WITHIN our own solar system."[2]

Geologist Eugene Shoemaker had pointed out that if the asteroid hit the ocean, the injection of water vapor into the atmosphere could increase the 'greenhouse' effect and warm the climate.[3]

Supernovas are rare events in the heavens. In a typical galaxy of a hundred billion stars, there is one supernova every 25 to 100 years.[4]

Iridium is produced and dispersed in supernova explosions.[5] Suns much like our own have been documented giving off major explosions, ordinary novae, and still remaining intact, like giant flares.[6]

Paleocene mammals are found below the iridium layer.[7] This means that the planet-destroying cataclysm that laid down the layer of iridium around the world was recent.

Scientists have discovered several examples of fossil plankton.[8] The delicacy of such tiny organisms having been petrified is astonishing and proves that their marine environment had been flash-frozen.[9]

The most common star in our galaxy is the red dwarf, seven out of ten of the closest stars are all red dwarfs. Proxima Centauri orbiting Alpha Centauri is the closest system to ours, but the red dwarf Proxima is by a factor of 100 too dim to be seen with the unaided eye. It orbits Alpha Centauri at 100,000 times the distance Earth orbits the Sun.[10] Therefore, our own system may have an orbiting red dwarf too and we would not know it.

Dr. Richard Muller in 1988 CE wrote, *"...the existence of Nemesis, the "death star," may be just what our species needs to make us appreciate that the real threat to our existence may not be other humans."*[11]

Carl Sagan wrote, *"...life on earth is intimately bound to stellar events. Human beings are here because of the paroxysms in dying stars thousands of light-years away."*[12]

1. Earth Under Fire p. 300; 2. Ibid p. 7-8; 3. Ibid p. 14; 4. Nemesis p. 52; 5. Nemesis p. 52; 6. Nemesis p. 62; 7. Nemesis p. 78; 8. Nemesis p. 79; 9. Nemesis p. 79; 10. Nemesis p. 109. 11. Nemesis p. 138; 12. The Cosmic Connection p. 262.

<u>5239 BCE</u> (-1344 AM): 7344 Before Armageddon/ 3000 Before Flood/ 1 Nemesis Cataclysm

This year begins the <u>Great Year</u> system of 600-year periods so popular among ancient chroniclers. It represents the beginning of Earth's geometrical timelines, the start of the <u>Nemesis Cataclysm timeline</u>, counting 2448 years three times over (7344 years) until the Anunnaki are destroyed in 2106 CE by the <u>Chief Cornerstone</u> at Armageddon when their power over mankind is broken. In 5239 BCE the original solar system is a differential binary system with a bright and smaller luminary, two stars, with the smaller orbiting the larger. The smaller star was known as the Daystar, having a series of planets orbiting it. From these was a gigantic planet known to the Sumerians as Nemesis X Object, a planet called Phoenix by ancient civilizations and our own world, Earth. There may have been more. During this period the other luminary, a bright star at night (because of the extreme distance between the sister stars), provided a soft blue illumination at night and also had orbiting it the planets we are familiar with today – planets that have never ceased orbiting it: Mercury, Venus, Mars, Electra (now the Asteroid Belt), Jupiter, Saturn, Uranus and Neptune. Our planet Earth was not part of this luminary's system until later, the result of a solar system cataclysm. The two Suns served as *"...the greater light to serve the day and the lesser light to serve the night,"* as found in Genesis, though this ancient fragment incorporated into the later Genesis writings has been mistaken with that of the moon. By this time, the world we call Earth is very old, with the heavens filled with brilliant stars attesting to its antiquity. Starlight is an <u>image</u> of prehistoric heaven, not an accurate visual representation of our Universe extant in real time. On Earth, prehistoric flora and fauna flourish under pristine biospheric conditions. The Anunnaki are the Builders, co-creators with the Eternal One, also called Watchers, Sons of God, Angels, and they are appointed to act as teachers and guardians over a sentient race of beings that they had made, a civilization antedating the creation of Homo sapiens; humanity. In this year, the Anunnaki sealed their fate in planning or starting designs deemed as rebellious to the Eternal One.

"He who fears the Anunnaki will lengthen his days."[1]

The Demiurge, one of the Seven Archons (Lords of Time), referred to in biblical passages as the God of This World, manipulated the holosphere and is now given 7344 years (2448x3) until he is imprisoned by the Unknown First Cause, the true Creator, represented as the Chief Cornerstone of the Builders.

"Create man that he may bear the yoke... let them slay a god, and let the gods with his flesh and his blood create. Let Ninhursag mix clay. God and man... united..."[2]

From an ancient tablet of the Assyrian city of Asher (circa 800 BCE) – *"When the earth had been brought forth, the earth had been fashioned. When the destinies of heaven and earth had been fixed... the Anunnaki, the great gods, seated themselves in the exalted sanctuary. And recounted among themselves what had been created... the Anunnaki, who fix the destinies, both groups of them, made answer to Enlil... let us slay (two) Lamga gods. With their blood let us create mankind. The service of the gods be their portion. For all times."*[3]

Saturn's moon Phoebe maintains a retrograde orbit very different than all of Saturn's other moons. It has 3% reflectivity making it difficult to see and it is perfectly round.[4] Approximately 120 miles in diameter, this satellite is possibly artificial.

The 4th planet from Sol was an enormous world remembered later as Tiamat, having 11 moons, its orbit located where the present asteroid belt lies. At this time, the Sol-orbiting planets were Mercury, Venus, Mars and Tiamat in the inner system instead of an asteroid belt. Earth itself did not orbit around Sol but instead orbited around its binary companion, Nemesis, along with Phoenix, Nemesis X Object, and other small worlds.

In December 1973, we launched the *Pioneer 10* spacecraft, which contained mankind's first communication to any extraterrestrial civilization. Supposedly, it departed our solar system traveling 7 miles per second, which even at such a velocity space is so vast that it will be 80,000 years before *Pioneer 10* even closes the distance to the nearest star.[5] Distances in space, as we've been led to believe, are so vast that it takes light photons traveling at 186,000 miles per second about 30,000 years to reach our world from the center of our own galaxy.[6] When astronomers observe deep-space objects far beyond the Milky Way, like other galaxies, they are not viewing it in real time... astronomers are gazing at an ever-changing panorama of the archaic past, at stellar objects as they appeared 900,000 to many million years ago. By the present paradigm foisted upon the public, the entire heavens could have died out hundreds of thousands of years ago and we would still not know it. That photons can travel such inconceivable distances through a medium saturated with other photons moving at various trajectories, subatomic particles acting as free radicals, water-ice crystals, gases, dust veils, nebulae, cometary detritus, rocks and asteroids, lunar bodies, planetoids, exoworlds, planets, other stars, event horizon anomalies and whatever else is out there is simply unbelievable, and this because it is untrue. The more one ponders the many incongruities of the Stella sphere the more evidence manifests that we are looking up into a manifold Dyson shell-like holosphere, either encapsulating our world with a false heavens or actually shelled around our entire solar system. This holospheric overlay produces a stellar canopy of visible and invisible gravitational bodies, optically there, but not physically extant, nodes of the holospheric net enshrouding us. This canopy of star-nodes is a holofield having layers of depth providing observers with the illusion of great distances and far off spaces; even apparent parallax is fabricated. The holography is either alive or of intelligence design and it is affected by and responds to human awareness. There are documented instances when the visible patterns of luminaries changed positions to conform to majority scientific theory or popular opinions.

Even our current primitive hologram technology demonstrates that the eye is easily deceived by the introduction of more and more intricate detail. Scientists cannot demonstrate that their observations are not made within a multi-tiered hologram.

Astronomers form models of how planets are created from star detritus that coalesces from great irregular masses or rock and metals. But they can't find any formative planets in their telescopes so they claim that our galaxy must be very old – a theory supported by a hypothesis. In buying time to show evidence in support of their theory, they added billions of years to the age of the galaxy. Hundreds of exoworlds have been viewed in this deceitful holosphere they call the heavens, but every one of them are spherical… fully developed planets. A new theory is not needed, rather, we are in need of new astronomers.

The Cambrian Explosion Event is a true mystery, for at least 10,000 new species suddenly appeared on earth having no evolutionary predecessors. Ivar Zapp and George Erikson remark, *"Nothing like these creatures existed before this explosion of life forms, and nothing new has been created since."*[7]

The original solar system was a differential binary – Nemesis and Sol. Prior to collapse of Nemesis, earth orbited Nemesis and it was home only to reptilians, amphibian, insectoid and marine creatures. Even in the prehistoric biosphere of this world under the Nemesis Sun, the avians were not birds as we know them, but reptiles. Orbiting Nemesis far away from its sister Sun, Sol, earth had no mammalian life forms.

Anunna commit a trespass in introducing some of their own DNA into primate mammals in an effort to create a worker race for mining who are adapted to Earth's biosphere.

Human civilization did not begin on planet earth. –David Icke[8]

Talmudists hold that the Creation of the world took place 5344 years before Christ.[9] This specific number is intriguing. Talmudists believed that Jesus was not the Messiah, but that the Messiah would come in the Last Days. Adding 2000 years to the 5344 years gives us 7344 years, the total timeline from 5239 BCE to 2106 CE.

Tiamat's dead body provided water that fell to the earth – a glaciosphere turned vaporous and torn away from a dead world to rain on ours.

Tiamat is not the dragon, but the mother of the dragons.[10]

Encyclopedia Americana, 1890, *"Of the actual magnitude and distance of the stars we know nothing. The diameter of the earth's orbit is 200,000,000 miles, yet we can detect no difference in their apparent places, viewed from the opposite points of this diameter. A change of place amounting only to a second would be detected by the accuracy of modern observations..."*[11]

"To learn the distances of the stars, it is first necessary to determine what is known as the star's parallax, or its angle of direction when viewed from two opposite points in the earth's orbit, and this is what renders the problem so extremely difficult, for nearly every star that has been examined for the purpose of learning its distance, has failed to show any parallax whatever, and even in the few instances where a parallax has been recognized, the angle has been found to be exceedingly small. No star in the heavens has a parallax equal to one second of arc, but all thus far determined are below even this small angle."[12]

Creation ex nihilo is a concept unknown in antiquity. From the human standpoint as recorded in the very oldest writings and traditions, the Beginning was the condition of the world already covered in primeval waters with many of these beliefs having attached to them the idea that these waters were the result of an early, prehistoric cataclysm.

A small island 40 miles off the southern tip of New Caledonia in the Pacific has about 400 unusual tumuli; ant hill shaped mounds of gravel and sand about 8 to 9 feet high with some 300 feet in diameter. There are 17 or so of these on New Caledonia. In the center of the mounds has been excavated upright pillars of cement, or cylinders. No burials, no bones, radiocarbon dating places them to about 5120 BCE.[13]

"History is generally considered that part of the past for which written documents exist." –Jake Page, *In the Hands of the Great Spirit*, pg 3. While this tenet is true, we can add a new dimension to the written word through the analysis of early traditions that comport with or expound upon the data derived from written records, as well as the discoveries that are made in archeology and chance discovery.

The analytical focus of *Chronicon* has been to comprehend the mathematical structures known in antiquity and the formulas employed in the introduction and maintenance of early calendars, time-keeping systems, methods of counting, or ways in which the passage of time was reckoned and to synchronize this information into a single linear chronology leading up to the present day.

Cavern dwelling of Petra was inhabited as far back as 5000 BCE.[14]

1. Babylonian inscription in Religion of Egypt and Assyria p. 389 cited in Sargon the Magnificent p. 104; 2. Adam When? p. 26-27, citing Alexander Heidel, The Babylonian Genesis, 1951; 3. Adam When? p. 27-28, citing Alexander Heidel, The Babylonian Genesis, 1951; 4. The Sirius Mystery p. 32; 5. The Cosmic Connection p. 18; 6. ibid. p. 52; 7. Atlantis in America p. 125; 8. And the Truth Shall Set You Free p. 12; 9. Ibid p. 50; 10. Atrahasis p. 98; 11. Is The Bible From Heaven p. 82-83 12. Is The Bible From Heaven p. 83; 13. Lost Cities of Ancient Lemuria & the Pacific p. 180; 14. Lost Cities and Ancient Mysteries of Africa and Arabia p. 27.

4687 BCE (-792 AM): 6792 Before Armageddon/ 2448 Before Flood/ 552 Nemesis Cataclysm/

The Anunnaki Homeworld is called Nemesis X Object, an immense planet orbiting both stars. The calendrics for this year denote that something momentous occurred on Nemesis X Object within Anunnaki society. The space-time periods of disaster align in this year. Nemesis X Object's orbit is 792 years and this year is 6000+792 years before Armageddon. This is 2448 years before the Great Flood, the number 2448 being the ancient Egyptian sum representing disaster, cataclysm, as will be seen in this chronology. This is the year 552 of the Nemesis Cataclysm, 552 years being a Phoenix Cycle known to the ancients as a period of time between catastrophes. Nemesis X Object and planet Phoenix both orbit the Daystar and travel along its ecliptic toward the other luminary, four billion miles away. They approach from the south of the system where Mercury and the other planets orbit along their own ecliptic path. These differential ecliptic planes (solar equators) formed an ecliptic cross that intersects exactly where Earth orbits this star today. The Daystar, Nemesis X Object, Phoenix, and Earth were in deep southern space underneath the solar system we call home today. This region of space to the south was known to the Sumerians as APSU, the Abyss or Deep. The original six signs of the Zodiac were viewed from this vantage point when Earth traveled a completely different ecliptic around the Sun's ancient sister star, formerly aligned with the Galactic Plane. The star patterns of the Zodiac do not fit their symbolic counterparts because the origin of the Zodiac antedates Earth's present position. Because Nemesis X Object orbited both Suns, it was called by the Sumerians as The Ferry and the Planet of the Crossing. Interestingly, the width of the Subterranean Chamber below the Great Pyramid is exactly 552 Pyramid Inches.

4639 BCE (-744 AM): 6744 Before Armageddon/ 2400 Before Flood/ 600 Nemesis Cataclysm/

The Eternal One permitted the Anunnaki access to the Records of Heaven, known also as the Tablets of Destinies or Tables of Heaven, archives concerning ancient heaven and the annals of the future, but they were admonished that they would be responsible for all they knew. The wise among the angelic hosts chose obedience and life, seeking no more than what they were inspired to learn. But others by diligent research into the future discovered that the Godhead would one day create His *own* human, not by the agency of divine fire, as He made the Anunnaki, but out of inferior clay. A third of the hosts of the Anunnaki took offense when they further discovered that this newer being made of mundane materials would actually play host to the Eternal Spirit of the Living God, than Man would become repositories of the Holy Spirit, the spiritual image of God. As the first beings that were created, the first born, the offended Anunnaki initiated the Daystar Rebellion and quit their services to their own pre-Adamic creations. The insurgents now blasphemously required themselves to be worshipped and began teaching their creations forbidden knowledge and the sciences of hybridization, arcane secrets that were to remain only within the order of the Watchers. The Anunnaki Homeworld fomented war between the planets of the Daystar. Nemesis X Object and Earth participated in this war, but if other worlds were involved, is not known. The Daystar planetary system began to lose its order and the brilliance of the Daystar began to wane. The sophisticated civilizations built by the Anunnaki for their creations were ruined and cities used advanced weapons against one another. As the Anunnaki readied themselves for a great war, colonies of pre-Adamites were sent out to mine materials from other uninhabited planets and moons. It was their intent to prepare for the coming of Man so they could eliminate the threat as soon as mankind emerged. As this year is precisely 744 years prior to the beginning of mankind's 6000 years of banishment that began in 3895 BCE, this year reflects the existence of the old Daystar in the Genesis text where we find the passage *"...two great lights,"* being 744, their gematrical value.[1]

Persian physician, astronomer and geographer Zakaria Al-Qazwini, a 13th century cosmographer, wrote, *"It is related in histories, that a race of Jinn, in ancient times, before the creation of Adam, inhabited the Earth, and covered it, the land and the sea, and the plains and the mountains; and the favors of God were multiplied upon them, and they had government, and prophecy and religion, and law; but they transgressed and offended, and opposed their prophets, and made wickedness to abound in the earth; whereupon God ,whose name be exalted, sent against them an army of angels, who took possession of the earth, and drove away the Jinn to the regions of the islands, and made many of them prisoners... "*[2]

1. *Stones and the Scarlet Thread, p. 36; 2. Legends of the Fire Spirits p. 7.*

4309 BCE (-414 AM): 6414 Before Armageddon/ 2070 Before Flood/ 930 Nemesis Cataclysm/ 1 Phoenix Year/

After 330 years of revolt and war, the 33.3% of the Anunnaki who rebelled and enslaved the pre-Adamites were pronounced guilty by the Word known to the Builders as the Chief Cornerstone, excommunicated from their divine appointments. Their ranks and stations in the heavens (Government of the Eternal One) were left abandoned, but their sentence was postponed, judgement delayed, and was only to be executed once the number of their fallen positions were filled by those they sought to unjustly slay... mankind. The Daystar went out, the luminary becoming dark after exploding and folding in on itself as a compressed star, or frozen star. In astronomical parlance, it became a Dark Star. Those planets nearest it were obliterated and have since filled the Kuiper Belt with detritus, the origin of those mysterious anomalies of rock and ice and dust we call <u>comets</u>. The outer world was hurled through space toward the surviving luminary, the star we call our Sun. Nemesis X Object drifted into a 792-year orbit, 732 years below the ecliptic and 60 years above the ecliptic plane, an orbit that would continue perfectly until 2106 CE, the year of Armageddon. Phoenix was totally destroyed and entered into a 138-year orbit <u>over</u> the Sun, spending much of its journey far out in the Kuiper Belt. Earth in this year began drifting toward the Sun and would not enter its present orbit for 270 years, the Earth completely frozen, the oceans solid ice. This lifeless drift is found in the Babylonian *Enuma Elish* text as *"...long were the days, years were added."*

The outer layers of the Daystar were ejected out into space to bombard its own planetary system and then heavily damage the planets and moons of our current solar system. After the initial explosion the internal core imploded and collapsed, this phenomenon changing it to become something between a black hole and a neutron star.[1] Astrophysicists assert that after a star explodes and loses much of its mass its gravitational influence plummets and the system loses its outer planets which are hurled into space.[2]

The Babylonian *Enuma Elish* texts, copied from older Sumerian documents, read that Earth was originally <u>from the Deep</u> (Abyss: south of present position orbiting Sun).[3] This early cosmological text records an ancient solar system cataclysm involving destruction of planets and their rearrangement. The Earth and its orbit, motion, and constellations of the Zodiac (ecliptic plane) as now seen from Earth, were not established until the Fifth Tablet, when the moon began orbiting Earth and it was ordained to *"determine the days."*[4] Amazingly, planet Phoenix's 45th visitation through the inner solar system was in 1902 CE when immense dust clouds and mud rained all over the world, the same year when the Babylonian cuneiform *Enuma Elish* records were translated into English and published with full photos of the ancient texts in an exhaustive work by L. W. King in London, by Luzac & Co. The Gnostic text *On the Origin of the World*, discovered in 1945 CE, reads that Phoenix was a witness against the powers of darkness, against the <u>angels</u>, and that it would endure until the Consummation [the End]. Phoenix was a witness in the heavens just as are the Sun and moon (identifying it as a celestial body). The Phoenix appears as a <u>sign</u> of what will occur in the end times when the Sun <u>will darken</u>, the moon ceases to shine, the oceans become agitated and chaos erupts.[5] This refers to the <u>Sixth Seal</u> of Revelation when planet Phoenix transits, darkening the Sun and initiating a pole shift in the year 2040 CE.

This 4309 BCE cataclysm, reflected in the Gnostic text *Trimorphic Protennoia*, shows that the gods (Anunnaki) were made fearful because their body of ascent (planet) was destroyed by a thunder in the Deep (southern space), caused by a great fire that overturned their Thrones (planets were called <u>Thrones</u> by the ancients). These Archons (Lords of Time: planetary motion) said, *"...our entire habitation has been shaken, and the entire circuit of our <u>path of ascent</u> [orbit] has been met with destruction, and the path upon which we go."*[6] This text depicts an orbit altered.

Mystic traditions published in *The Holy Tablets*, which cite thousands of references to Sumerian and ancient Near East texts, claim that the world was inhabited <u>before</u> Adam but was destroyed when a <u>dust cloud hid the Sun</u> and meteorites fell upon Earth. This ruination is why Genesis reads, *"And there was darkness over the face of the <u>Deep</u>."*[7]

At this time in 4309 BCE most of the Anunnaki were trapped upon their own homeworld, Nemesis X Object, but others were trapped upon a lunar body called the Dark Satellite. Both Nemesis X Object and the Dark Satellite will directly bear upon the course of human history, as they near the Earth and the Anunnaki are able to travel between the two for short periods. The entire interplanetary civilization built by the Anunnaki is destroyed, including the animals they had made that we refer to as dinosaurs, gigantic reptilian and amphibian lifeforms that flourished on Earth when Earth orbited the Daystar. Frozen solid and flooded, the entire planet became a fossil and the Eternal One cursed the Anunnaki to assume the physical forms of their own creations. When the Anunnaki appear on Earth, they appear as reptilian or amphibian with large eyes and sickly bodies.

The calendrics for this year are intriguing. As this is the 930th year of the Nemesis Cataclysm timeline, it parallels the age of Adam who died in his 930th year. 930 is the product of 792 and 138, the orbital periods of Nemesis X Object and Phoenix.

Folklorist Else Christensen studied ancient European calendrical systems and determined that the year 4311 BCE began a calendar, the

Zodiacal Age of the Bull.[8] This is a very amazing finding, for 4311 BCE is only 2 years variance from 4309 BCE. In context of over 63 centuries, Christensen's calculation is virtually precise.

Charles Fort in 1919 CE wrote, *"If other worlds have ever in the past had relations with this earth, they were attempts… to extend themselves, by colonies upon this earth… or assimilate, indigenous inhabitants of this earth… parent worlds and their colonies."*[9]

Phoenix is a word etymologically related to epiphany: Epi and Phanes, or wonder in the sky.[10]

Typhon is also rendered as Typhaon (Ti-phaon-ix).

Typhon in Liddel and Scott's *Greek Lexicon* is explained as *"a type of comet,"* or a moving star,[11] its cognates, Typhlos, is to blind in the sense of being misty, darkened, and the verb Typhloo means to wrap in smoke.[12]

Typhon of the Greeks was said to be so big its head reached the stars, its wings so broad they blocked out the Sun.[13]

Phoenician Typhon was Tzephŭn.[14] (Phoenix)

Hesiod in *Theogany*, 870 seq. calls it the *"…dragon-headed Typhoeus."*[15]

Typhon was called the Prince of Darkness.[16]

In Egypt, Tiamat is the Goddess Maat, of Law and Order in the universe.[17]

Dragon/Tiamat/Primordial cataclysm at Creation – Psalms 89:9, 74:13, Isaiah 51:9, 27:1, Job 26:12, 2 Peter 3:5

Egyptian Kneph is equivalent to spirit.[18] Kneph = Phoenix

Job 26:12-13 is about Phoenix. Palmer wrote that *"Delitzch understands it to be the dragon in the heavens which by winding round the Sun causes it to be eclipsed."*[19]

Leviathon derives from that *"Dragon which fights against the Sun."*[20]

This freezing period began a 414-year period to the pole shift of 3895 BCE. The Greenland ice-cores mark a period of bitter cold that lasted some four hundred years.[21] Ian Wilson believed this four-century long *"cold snap"* was about 5800 BCE,[22] however, the 3895 BCE Lithospheric displacement and collapse of the Vapor Canopy in 2239 BCE, called the Great Flood, altered the ice-core data. Further, as will be shown, the ice-core date was already 36-61 years off from the global cooling caused by immense volcanism in 1687 BCE.

Sitchin notes the discovery of a clay tablet found in the ruins of the Royal Library in Nineveh. It is an Assyrian copy of an earlier Sumerian technolithic circular disk tablet, admittedly a most baffling document bearing geometric shares unseen on any other ancient relics all designed with considerable precision. Triangles, arrows, intersecting lines and an amazing ellipse, brought to attention of the British Royal Society, 1880 CE by R.H.M. Bosanquet and A.H. Sayce who concluded that it suggested measurements, *"...to bear some technical meaning."*[23] Sitchin conveys that it is an atronomical document involving all 360 degrees of the heavens, mentioning planets, stars and *"...a celestial body called APIN,"* Also, vapor clouds.[24](Note: A-PIN is similar to Egyptian PN-God and PHOEN-IX)

The Gnostic cosmology held that our cosmos had a fiery Sun and a Black Sun.[25]

This cataclysm was at 930 years of the Nemesis Cataclysm Timeline, from 5239 BCE. In the 6th-4th centuries BCE the records of this major destruction were kept in Babylon and were copied by exiled Jews who borrowed passages to their liking and altered the original texts which reads, *"...the destruction of the world [Adamu] in the 930th year,"* to their fictive Genesis account that reads that Adam died in his 930th year. Adam and Eve are Jewish versions of Babylonian passages from the badly misunderstood records of the Old World concerning a period when the first modern humans [Adamu] thrived in a civilization that endured 930 years and ended abruptly in disaster.

This worldwide ruin is found in Jeremiah 4:23-26, the earth *"...without form and void... all cities destroyed."* All cosmogenesis traditions from antiquity have earth born from a chaos [disruption from a previous order] linked to evil that involved the visitation of a celestial dragon [frightening body in the sky].

Phoenix Year timeline is 2070 years to the Great Flood (2239 BCE), the exact midpoint between these disasters being 3274 BCE (621 Annus Mundi), the year Enoch/Enki was conceived, the famous antediluvian chronologist, scientist, mathematician, architect, prophet, scribe and ruler and builder of Giza. The Phoenix Weapon in the sky is the key to all world chronology.

A great many Old World traditions convey that the first people were born in a world of ice, or from the body/blood of an ice/frost giant. The human race is a living DNA repository designed solely by the Anunnaki to enslave spiritual beings in carnal bodies. The present human race has intentionally had entire gene sequences deactivated [latent DNA] to impede our ability to recognize that reality is governed by fixed protocols of a prison-like containment field disguised as a universe. Human DNA is the transgenic combination of 66.6% terrestrial mammalian DNA and 33.3% Anunnaki DNA.

Anunnaki employ world-moving technology using the Phoenix Weapon resulting in a pole shift/or lithospheric displacement, oceans slip from the basins, widespread flooding, volcanism, wholesale destruction. No Sun was seen in the sky at this time for it had not yet been *"born,"* according to the oldest traditions. The vault of the sky was a vapor canopy and the Ancients described it as like an ocean above. From the North Pole extending across the world to 30 degrees south of the Equator the earth was frozen. South of this, marsupial and mammalian life forms thrived. Neanderthal in scattered groups survived as Cro-Magnon communities also lived, mostly in underground dwellings.

The Phoenix can no longer be regarded as a dead world on a highly elliptical orbit because its reappearance in the month of May, over and over again, documented over thousands of years, as it reappears every 138 years, necessitates the existence of a controlled and local phenomenon, which is a part of the vast mechanism of the sky. The Phoenix Weapon protocol is known by its effect – population control, inducing retardation of human development, to destroy local and very enlightened populations or whole hemispheres, and in some few cases, the entire world. The reader who finishes *Chronicon* from 5239 BCE all the way to 2040 CE will have no doubt that the Phoenix is an intelligently designed weapon hidden in our local sky to repeatedly maintain checks on human population levels, to destroy the works of men and intentionally BURY THEM IN MUD from the clear sky, to initiate arrested development and induce volcanic resurfacing, which entombs prior land surfaces, while also bringing to the surface harvestable deep-earth metals and minerals. The chief design of the Phoenix phenomenon is to mask the abduction of human populations and materials from our world under the guise of natural disasters – the introduction of chaos to keep the human victims ignorant that they are being harvested.

The Heliopolitan cosmology of Egypt as revealed in Edfu reliefs held that BEFORE the appearance of the NETERU [Ten Divinities started 3439 BCE to 2239 BCE, a dynasty of Ten Kings] the PN-god appeared in *"...some kind of violent conflict which brought to a close the first period of Creation. An enemy appeared in the form of a serpent [Dragon] known as the Great Leaping One... as a consequence of this mass devastation the first inhabitants all die, and darkness returns to the world."*[26] Egyptian tradition provides no date, but the PN-god is the same as the Phoen-deity, or the *Phoenix*. It brings death and decay and the earth vanishes into the watery NUN of Chaos and perpetual dark.[27] The PN-god is also called the Falcon and The Winged One,[28] the Winged Disk of the Near East being the greatest symbol for Phoenix and the most widely misinterpreted symbol EVER. Throughout thousands of official translations and reference books in hundreds of languages for the last three centuries all so-called authorities claim the Winged Disk seen so prolifically throughout the reliefs and art of the ancient world, was simply a symbol for the Sun... an absolute LIE.

We have unique confirmation of the PN-god association to the Phoenix from the ancient Sumerian astronomical tablets. *"When APIN reaches the path of the Sun, there will be a famine of cattle, there will be want. When a planet and APIN stand facing one another, there will be an invasion of the enemy."*[29] Translators are confused, some thinking that APIN is a reference to Mars but in the same text Mars is affirmatively identified by them as Lul-a.[30] The explanatory notes reveal that APIN appears three times and scholars were confused, thinking it was referring to Mars but the only association is that Mars is a ***red planet***. The confusion was ancient, for the tablets under APIN even have explanatory notes.[31]

Heliopolis was the City of the Sun, a metropolis of learning with universities and libraries known to Greece, Anatolia, Ionia, Crete, Phoenicia, Canaan, Syria, Mesopotamia, Elam and India. In this City of the Sun in Egypt at an old temple was located the Mansion of the Phoenix, called benben, where astronomer-priests taught the Heliopolitan concept of reoccurring cycles of time connected to the archaic Bennu Bird, *"...the purple-plumed Phoenix of Greek tradition."*[32] The Bennu Bird was celestial and its appearance *"...signaled the death of the First Time [Zep Tepi], the Golden Age of the gods (5239 BCE to 4309 BCE) and the commencement of a New World Epoch."*[33] Andrew Collins wrote that each time the Bennu Bird was seen to return over Heliopolis it marked the end of an Aeon and the commencement of the next.[34]

Harold Wilkins in his work, *Mysteries of Ancient South America*, wrote, *"Mr. H. S. Bellamy, an authority on myths of the Moon in the ancient world, supposes that the Book of Revelation... is really a history of the Great Cataclysm, and enshrines, in mystic and cryptic language, some ancient story of an earlier, pre-Lunar satellite of the earth approaching close to the earth."*[35] Bellamy cites the theory of Austrian engineer Hans Horbiger of Vienna – *"When the satellite drew near to the earth, it shown with a brilliant light reflected from the Sun, falling on a thick coating of ice – the glaciosphere. This split and fell on the earth, exposing a layer of red earth, which, in turn, fell on the earth in a rain like blood."*[36] Bellamy's pre-Lunar catastrophe was in 4309 BCE, for the Moon appeared in 4039 BCE.

Phoenix is a governor, a weapon on a planetary scale hidden in the sky, local and not revisiting our world every 138 years from some long impossible orbital journey, but activating when its designed programming protocols instruct it to. Every single appearance of the Phoenix that caused ruin and desolation throughout human history is perfectly found in the chronometrical measurements of the Great Pyramid of Giza in architectural features that NO OTHER pyramids in the world replicate.

The Phoenix Weapon destroyed a thriving human civilization and its survivors are known to us as Cro-Magnon, a human breed physically, mentally and genetically superior to any Homo sapiens today. This began a 270-year darkness.

The megafauna of the Old World died – giant bison, horse, sloths, enormous lions, dire wolves, gigantic bears, sabretooth tigers, mammoths and wooly rhinosaurus – their millions of bodies found deposited in heaps by water, buried in sediment, many in remarkable states of preservation.

The death of the megafauna could have been caused by a pole shift that froze to death the millions of animals in northern Asia and Siberia, however, that the same fields of frozen animals are found in the opposite hemisphere in North America reveals that a polar shift or lithospheric displacement is not the answer. Only the sudden flooding and polar freezing of the water canopy collapse answers all the evidence.

Baffin Island has a huge forest of trees now petrified under the ice.[37]

Huge herds of wooly mammoths and rhinos died of cold in central Alaska.[38]

Geologists agree that in ancient times most of Nevada was an inland sea, and Lake Tahoe, Walker and Pyramid Lake are but surviving relics of this earlier body of water. The region has yielded up the remains of the huge ground sloths, mastodons and rhinos. Arrowheads, ground sloth skulls and hides, and well-preserved shreds of hide and course hair not yet decomposed are causing some to assume a date of about 3000 BCE. Evidence that sloths had been domesticated has also been found.[39]

1. New Worlds in the Cosmos p. 97; 2. Ibid p. 100; 3. Lines 1-3 of First Tablet, Enuma Elish p. 3; 4. Enuma Elish p. 79; 5. The Nag Hammadi Library pgs. 186-188; 6. Ibid pgs. 517-518; 7. The Holy Tablets 1:76 p. 5 col. 2; 8. The Nature of Asatrup. 204; 9. Book of the Damned pgs. 171-172; 10. Comets: Swords of Heaven p. 15; 11. The Sirius Mystery p. 226; 12. Ibid p. 226; 13. Flying Serpents and Dragons p. 32; 14. Babylonian Influence on the Bible and Popular Beliefs p. 56; 15. Babylonian Influence on the Bible and Popular Beliefs p. 93; 16. Pagan and Christian Creeds p. 49; 17. How the Sun-God Reached America p. 13; 18. The Popol Vuh p. 69; 19. Babylonian Influence on the Bible and Popular Beliefs p. 38; 20. Ibid p. 39; 21. Before the Flood p. 133; 22. Ibid p. 133; 23. 1. The 12th Planet p. 273; 24. Ibid p. 273; 25. The Mammoth Book of Lost Symbols p. 419; 26. Gods of Eden: Collins p. 175; 27. Gods of Eden: Collins p. 175; 28. ibid p. 187; 29. The Reports of the Magicians and Astrologers p. liv; 30. Ibid p. liv; 31. Ibid p. liv; 32. Gods of Eden: Collins p. 134, 150; 33. Gods of Eden: Collins p. 150; 34. ibid p. 150; 35. Mysteries of Ancient South America p. 32; 36. ibid p. 32; 37. Lost Cities of North and Central America p. 451; 38. Lost Cities of North and Central America p. 451; 39. Lost Cities of North and Central America p. 492.

4291 BCE (-396 AM): 6396 Before Armageddon/ 2052 Before Flood/ 948 Nemesis Cataclysm/ 18 Phoenix Year

Nemesis X Object enters the inner solar system 18 years after the destruction of the Daystar and binary system in 4309 BCE. Nemesis X Object, over 8 times the mass of Earth, catapults the frozen Earth toward the Sun, which it will begin to orbit in 252 years, positioned between the orbits of Venus and Mars. This year is 396 years before Man's banishment in 3895 BCE, 396 being half the orbit of Nemesis X Object's 792 years. Later, the Anunnaki will descend and rule over mankind, but this Dynasty will end violently 2052 years later with the Great Flood, mirroring the future year of 2052 CE when the Anunnaki Seven Kings begin their rulership of post-apocalyptic Earth. 4291 BCE is 6336 years (792x8) before the Anunnaki Invasion in 2046 CE as described in the Revelation text. This year is 4320 years (1080x4) before the start of the Chief Cornerstone's ministry in 30 CE, the one who is called Christ. Nemesis X Object ascends out of the Deep, passes over the Sun's ecliptic, and begins its 60-year journey north of the Sun.

4236 BCE (-341 AM):

This is the scholarly-accepted start-date for the Egyptian Long-Chronology.[1] This is only 73 years after the pre-Adamic destruction of Earth.

1. Civilization or Barbarism? p. 281.

4231 BCE (-336 AM): 6336 Before Armageddon/ 1992 Before Flood/ 1008 Nemesis Cataclysm/ 78 Phoenix Year

Nemesis X Object exits the inner solar system after 60 years north of the ecliptic on a highly elliptical orbit. This is 6336 years (792x8) before the Chief Cornerstone vanquishes the Anunnaki in 2106 CE at Armageddon.

4171 BCE (-276 AM): 6276 Before Armageddon/ 1932 Before Flood/ 1068 Nemesis Cataclysm/ 138 Phoenix Year

Planet Phoenix enters the inner solar system completing its 138-year orbit passing through the system on its way back to the Kuiper Belt. Earth is not yet orbiting the Sun, but is still lost in space, and 132 years away from assuming an orbit between Venus and Mars.

4104 BCE (-209 AM):

In 222 CE Diogenes Laertius wrote that the Egyptians claimed that their histories spanned back 48,863 *"years"* from Alexander the Great.[1] This is a lunar code that is interpreted by dividing this sum by 13 lunar months. Counting from 345 BCE, this places the start date at 4104 BCE, but counting from 331 BCE, when Alexander defeated the Persians, then the date would be 4089 BCE.

1. Secret Cities of Old South America, p. 56.

4040 BCE (-145 AM): 6145 Before Armageddon/ 1801 Before Flood/ 1199 Nemesis Cataclysm/ 269 Phoenix Year

The temple of Dendera in Egypt was built by the Ptolemys, on the site of an older structure, the newer temple following the older plan, which was built to commemorate ancient zodiacal knowledge. Admitting he does not know why, Paul A. LaViolette, Ph.D., shows that the Dendera zodiac encodes in our calendar the date 4040 BCE.[1] This is only 1 year off from the actual 4039 BCE date.

1. Earth Under Fire, p. 81.

4039 BCE (-144 AM): 6144 Before Armageddon/ 1800 Before Flood/ 1200 Nemesis Cataclysm/ 270 Phoenix Year/ 1 Capture of Luna

Planet Earth drifts into the solar system after 270 years frozen solid, free of the Dark Star's gravitational hold. Earth begins to orbit the Sun tucked unusually between the orbits of Venus and Mars, which disrupts the equidistant mathematical distribution of the planets as measured from the surface of the Sun, revealed in the Titius-Bode Law. Earth's distance from the Sun reveals that it is an intruder planet. The planets already orbiting the Sun were priorly damaged by detritus from the explosion of the Daystar. At this time, there are Anunnaki on Earth and they participate in Earth's renovation.

Ancient Akkadian cosmology has the moon pre-existing the Sun.[1] This is confirmed in the Egyptian *Turin Papyrus*[2] and Mexican traditions claim that Venus existed before the Sun.[3] The earliest known Sumerian tablets (circa 3500 BCE) recall that when the gods called, the Anunnaki came to Earth and found it covered in dense cloud cover – *"Daylight did not shine, moonlight had not emerged."*[4] Amazingly, according to the Vedic *Rig-Veda*, the proximity of a heat-source to a water-covered world was what brought Earth back to life.[5] Once in orbit around the hot Sun the Earth began to roll, what we term as rotational spin on its axis as found in Genesis 1 where *"...the evening and the morning were the first day."* This spinning begins the rapid renovation of Earth as it thaws out. Billions of marine, amphibian and reptilian lifeforms emerge from their dormant stasis after the world had been quick-frozen 270 years earlier.

The Anunnaki create humankind at the end of a 600-year period according to the writings in *The Holy Tablets*.[6] This conforms nicely to the 600-year periods of the Nemesis Cataclysm. In fact, it was long ago taught that a *"divine man"* would arise every 600 years throughout world history.[7] As will be shown, several famous figures throughout history were born at these intervals. Mankind, according to the *Enuma Elish*, was created in the Sixth Tablet[8], just as in Genesis humans were made on the Sixth day.

The start of Man in this year is encoded in the first verse of Genesis, which reads, *"In the beginning,"* the word *"beginning"* derived from a root (kedem) which has the gematrical value of 144, carrying with it the idea of eternalness.[9] This year of 4039 BCE is 144 years before

Mankind is banished from paradise (from the old Persian, *pardis*, meaning "walled enclosure"), also called Eden, in 3895 BCE. This begins a 6000-year timeline to Man's Redemption in 2106 CE with the return of the Chief Cornerstone.

Homo sapiens is a genetically-improved creation by the Anunnaki from pre-existing lifeforms made extinct in the cataclysm of 4309 BCE. But this time the Eternal One, through His Word, intervened and breathed the spirit into mankind, thus making humanity in the <u>image of God</u>. This took away the total control of the Anunnaki, who sought to create a planetary slave race of workers. For this reason, the Anunnaki, as Watchers, have regarded their own Maker, the Eternal One, as a thief. Humanity would have the knowledge necessary to discern between <u>good and evil</u>. The only command given to humanity is *"... be fruitful, and multiply and <u>replenish</u> the Earth."* It is this statement that reveals that Earth was formerly inhabited. Man's creation on the 6th day denotes his appearance after a period of 144 hours (6 days). The units of measurement known as the day, the month and the year are measurements of mechanical time, the axial rotation of the Earth, the revolution of the moon around the Earth, and that of the Earth around the Sun. But the period called the <u>week</u> was by divine appointment, not represented by mechanical time. Seven days.

The Great Pyramid's surface-sloping angle, with its casing blocks in place, was precisely 51°51', which matches geometrically the true length of the year in <u>Sabbaths</u> (7-day periods). The year is 51.51 weeks at this time, being <u>360 days</u>. The year will remain 360 days in length until another disaster in 713 BCE, which alters Earth's orbit to 365.25 days. This year of 4039 BCE begins Earth's <u>Capture of Luna</u>, a timeline of our planet discovered by David Davidson in the geometrical measurements between the Great Pyramid's four cornerstones and published in his enormous book, *The Great Pyramid: Its Divine Message*, published in 1924 CE. Davidson declares that the astronomical chronology in the Great Pyramid's measurements began in 4040 BCE and ends in 2045 CE, which would be the end of a timeline involving our planet. He is only 1 year off (4039 BCE & 2046 CE). Davidson knew nothing about the Nemesis X Object or about Earth being an <u>intruder planet</u>. As will be found in this research, in 2046 CE Earth will be moved away from its current orbital path around the Sun and this transposition will alter the length of the day and year. The Great Pyramid's <u>Capture of Luna</u>

timeline measures the 6084 years between 4039 BCE and 2046 CE where Earth remains in a stable orbit along the Sun's ecliptic. It will not remain here.

So the year 4039 BCE is Year One of the Great Pyramid's Orbital Chronology, which is 6084 years in duration, lasting until Earth is again removed from its orbit in 2046 CE (5940 AM). The Orbital Chronology of the pyramid monument was discovered in the 1920s by David Davidson.

This event was the 1200th year [600+600] of the Nemesis Cataclysm timeline and 600 years before the 3439 BCE appearance of the Watchers (Anunnaki) and 1200 years before the 2839 BCE start of the Nephilim Dynasty (Anunnaki Dynasty timeline), which was itself 600 years before the Great Deluge in 2239 BCE.

Throughout *Chronicon* will be revealed evidence that the Moon image in the sky is merely a picture and either does not exist materially or is a holographic camouflage disguising something else like an occupied superconstruction.

4039 BC is Anno Luna, or Year One of the Moon Chronology (Capture of Luna timeline).

Even as early as 1890 CE, Alex Gleason noted that the Theory of Gravity does not explain the perfect lunations of the Moon. The Moon's orbit is too perfect, unchanging, and the position officially is that gravity would cause drag and pull from other planets that is just nonexistent.[10] The firstborn son of the Anunna god Enlil was Nannar, or Moon, where Sumerian texts reveal the god Enki obtained the seed material to make mankind. This seed was connected to a cataclysm involving the destruction of Tiamat. In the Near East after the Great Deluge (2239 BCE), the Moon was called Sin.[11] The oldest belief in recorded history concerning the origin of humanity holds that mankind came from the Moon. For this reason, after the Anunna civil war began, Sin [the Anunna occupants from the Moon] sided with the human benefactor Enki, which incited Enlil to declare that those who opposed him were Sinners… or, of the Moon.[12]

Genesis 1:2 *"The spirit of God [Kneph=Phenc, or Phoenix] moved over the Deep (waters)."* This appearance of the Moon was 6 years before the appearance of Phoenix (Kneph) in 4033 BCE, this number, 6, being recorded in ancient Semitic traditions as being the stages of the Creation in 6 days, or cycles or years.

Ancient American cosmological beliefs held that in the beginning the god Huracan [origin of hurricane], a mighty god of wind, passed over the waters of Chaos in the form of a huge bird [Phoenix], thus bringing earth into being.[13] Lewis Spence's notes in *The Popul Vuh* record that in many ancient American traditions, *"...the central idea of Creation is supplied by the brooding of a Great Bird over the dark primeval waste of waters."*[14]

1. Gerald Massey Lectures p. 119; 2. Ibid p. 119; 3. Ibid p. 120; 4. Flying Serpents and Dragons p. 61; 5. History in Quotations p. 25; 6. The Oxford Illustrated Companion p. 104, The Holy Tablets, The Shabaat p. 99, col. 1 and 4:71-73, p. 173 col. 1; 7. The Christ Conspiracy p. 338; 8. Enuma Elish p. 87; 9. Beginnings: The Sacred Design p. 172; 10. Is the Bible From Heaven? Is the Earth a Globe? p. 256; 11. Our Occulted History pgs. 157-158; 12. Our Occulted History p. 158; 13. Babylonian Influence p. 9, citing Myths of the New World p. 210, D.G. Brinton; 14. The Popol Vuh, the Mythic and Heroic Sagas of the Kichés of Central America, p.31.

4033 BCE (-138 AM): 6138 Before Armageddon/ 1794 Before Flood/ 1206 Nemesis Cataclysm/ 276 Phoenix Year

Planet Phoenix enters the inner solar system, completing its 138-year orbit, passing through the system on its way back out to the Kuiper Belt. This was 6 years (72 months) after the appearance of Man, counting 1656 months (414x4) or 138 years to Man's Banishment from Eden in 3895 BCE.

Phoenix (Phenc=Noph) passes close to earth six years after the 4039 BCE appearance of Luna. Phoenix nudges the earth-moon system to begin rolling together. Jews called this the six days of creation.[1]

1. Lost Civilizations.

4004 BCE (-109 AM): 6109 Before Flood/ 1765 Before Flood/ 1235 Nemesis Cataclysm/ 305 Phoenix Year/ 35 Capture of Luna

This has become recognized as the date of the Creation to Christians, as published in multitudes of study Bibles and books, and having its origin with the chronological research of James Ussher's *Annals of the World* (1658). The date is 109 years off, like so many of Ussher's old world dates. The correct date is 3895 BCE – not for the Creation, but for the initiation of a New Calendar representing a New World post-Cataclysm governing of a new thing – modern humans. As will be shown, Ussher made an error of 108-110 years on many ancient world dates by wrongly calculating Julian/Gregorian BCE dates, while getting many of the corresponding Annus Mundi dates correct.

3895-3112 BCE

**3895 BCE (1 AM): 6000 Years of Man's Banishment Begins/ 6000
Before Flood/ 1656 Before Flood/ 1344 Nemesis Cataclysm/
414 Phoenix Year/ 144 Capture of Luna**

In Man's 144th year in the Walled Enclosure (Paradise) a chief among
the Anunnaki Watchers, a Seeing One or Interpreter, also called a serpent
in Genesis, misleads mankind into doubting the Word of the Eternal
One. Humanity in Eden had been given the discretion to live free from
doubt and constraints, but by listening to the Interpreter, mankind fell
under the power of those that defined for them good and evil. Once
mankind's eyes were opened (sinister intent of the Anunnaki), humanity
was no longer *beyond* good and evil, and was from that point onward
a slave to their own consciousness. Now with his conscience as his
guide, mankind is cursed to condemn himself. With their eyes opened,
according to a Gnostic text, the first humans *"...saw their makers,
they loathed them since they were beastly forms."*[1] This supports the
finding that the Anunnaki were changed by the Eternal One to mirror
their original creations, the reptiles and amphibians of the prehistoric
period. Man is cursed and sent out into the Earth for 6000 years until the
return of the Chief Cornerstone who the Builders (Anunnaki) rejected.
The 6000 years will be reconfirmed in several astonishing ways in this
research. The 6000th year is 2106 CE, the exact year that Nemesis X
Object, the Anunnaki homeworld, will pass close to Earth on its way
back out of the inner solar system.

Banished into the wild, mankind attempts to go back to the Walled
Enclosure but the appearance of a *"fiery flaming sword"* prevents
this, held by an angelic guardian. The account has promoted much
confusion. Celestial bodies like comets and unknown planets that gave
off tails in the sky were referred to as swords as seen in Scripture, in the
writings of Josephus and Pliny.[2] In this year planet Phoenix entered the
inner solar system, completing its 138-year orbit, passing through the
system on its way back to the Kuiper Belt. It is the visual appearance
of planet Phoenix that signaled the start of the 6000-year timeline and
set in stone the association in antiquity between comets and celestial

bodies and JUDGEMENT ON EARTH. This judgment will culminate when Phoenix initiates an apocalyptic event darkening the Sun in 2040 CE and initiating a pole shift disaster that is referred to in Revelation as the Sixth Seal. Another name for Phoenix was Typhon, a name preserving [Phoen]ix as seen in Ty[phon]. Plutarch relates that Typhon was reddish and Massey wrote that the ancients wrote often about a celestial body with a red tail.[3]

The palm tree long ago was a symbol of the reckoning of time, and in Hebrew, the palm is Phenice, with ancient roots resolving to 'fo en ix', or One Great Fire.[4] The palm branch was a symbol for time and periodicity. Horapollo wrote that it was adopted as a symbol for the month. Time was reckoned by plucking off the shoots on a palm branch.[5] In Assyria the palm tree was the Tree of Life, also identifiable as a flaming column, and it is found often encoiled by a serpent. The palm [Phoenix] merges all of these concepts.[6] Phoenix is the planet of chronology.

That Adam was 144 years old when banished is reflected in the Kabbalistic tradition, and he is assigned the number 144.[7] Adam in Hebrew is ADM. The A has a value of 1, the D is 4 and M is 40, but zero has no value. The sum of ADM is thus 1.4.4.[8] In old Assyrian and Akkadian tablets the word ADAM is found used as a proper name.[9] The Curse humanity suffers is elaborated on by the prophet Ezekiel, who wrote that the Four Judgements God employs against mankind to curb sin and rebellion throughout world history are SWORD, FAMINE, PLAGUE, and WILD BEASTS.[10]

This year begins a 1948-year countdown to the birth of Abraham, who will father many nations. This 1947 BCE birth counts another 1948 years to 1 CE, the start of a whole different calendrical system. In the 1948th year of this new Common Era (Anno Domini) calendar the nation of Israel will be reestablished. Additionally, this is the year 1344 of the Nemesis Cataclysm timeline, 1344 being a product of 792 and 552. The Nemesis X Object's orbit is 792 years and Phoenix Cycles dreaded in antiquity were 552 years, or 4 orbits of 138 years each. In the year 1860 CE, W. Morgan calculated the Druid precessional system, which began when the equinox occurred in the first point of Taurus, his calculation being 3903 BCE.[11] This is an amazing feat, for in over 57½ centuries Morgan was only 8 years off. After extensive research of the biblical records, the *Book of Jasher* and *Assyrian Eponyms*, chronologist Stephan Jones in his *Secrets of Time* published that this year, 3895 BCE, was Year One – so highly regarded by the Ancient World. This 6000-year timeline had NOTHING to do with the Creation, but is a fixed <u>astronomical chronology</u> that began with the appearance of planet Phoenix in 3895 BCE, the first time humans witnessed it, and ends in 2106 CE when Nemesis X Object exits the solar system. The geometrical framework of world history unfolds within the parameters of the visitations of these two <u>intruder planets</u>.

Charles Fort in 1919 CE wrote, *"I think we're property, I should say we belong to something; that once upon a time, this earth was No-Man's Land, that other worlds explored and colonized here, and fought among themselves for possession, but that now it's owned by something; that something owns this Earth – all others warned off."*[12]

Major flooding of the Near East detected in strata dated to about 4000 BCE,[13] however, this could be the 3895 BCE pole shift.

The *"dried-out landmasses"* in the Genesis creation is a correct rendering for the waters *"were gathered into one place, ... "* (Yabashah)[14] This is 1948 years to 1948 BCE (Abraham's birth and first regnal year of King Nimrod [Sargon I of Akkad]), which is 1948 years to the Anno Domini (Common Era) Calendar, and 1948 CE being the year of Israel's national rebirth.

3895 to 3439 BCE Post-Pole shift Neolithic Restart (pre-3895 BCE cultures ended by upheavals).

The Fall of Man idea was an old Babylonian sin doctrine, having been diffused into many ancient religious faiths – strongly in Judaism, then Christianity. Sin was disobedience to the gods (Anunnaki). The earliest Mesopotamian records relate that humanity was created to be a slave species, that present Homo sapiens was the last created of two or more trial species from distant antiquity. Velikovsky wrote that the Talmudic texts teach that the world was successively destroyed and inhabited before Adam.[15] When in the 6th to 5th centuries BCE, the Jews came into contact with the magnificent and old libraries of Babylon. They borrowed from chronological annals and composed their Genesis, corrupting the original story of Eden. They invented Adam and Eve and wrote that by disobedience their eyes were opened – they were ashamed of their nakedness. But the true original records concerned the *Adamu*, which was a word for mankind, and the revolt of men against the Anunnaki taskmasters was due to his recognition of his slave status.[16] Humans rebelled from the labor and escaped a walled enclosure (garden) and the Anunnaki promised that mankind would die. Further evidence of Jewish manipulation of Babylonian date-annals concerns the rabbinical *Book of Jasher*. In Babylon, the Jews read of a disaster and ominous "darkening of the Sun" at the death and banishment of the Adamu, prompting the Jews to write in their narrative that at the death of Adam *"...the Sun darkened."* The Creation story and account of the Fall of Man involve the *"fiery revolving sword"* and cherub that appeared after mankind was cursed to die by the Elohim (gods: Anunnaki) contain elements of an almost forgotten cataclysm, later moralized by Babylonian and Jewish religionists. Velikovsky in his manuscript, *In the Beginning*, demonstrates that the loss of Eden and curse concerns a major *"civilization destroying catastrophe."* Later, the few survivors did not even know their own origin.[17]

The borrowing of Babylonian annals is most evident in the years assigned to the Great Flood (1656 AM: 2239 BCE) and the great quakes of 2208 AM (1687 BCE), both disasters recording a strange darkening of the Sun and both being 552 years apart. All three dates (3895, 2239 BCE, 1687 BCE) are 552 years apart or multiples of 552 years, being Phoenix destructions, and were used by the Jews to legitimize their forged histories.

The Eden story recalled in earlier times the appearance of a hero, a benefactor, a figure who promised mankind that he would help, one who told early humanity the truth and informed them that their deceitful Anunnaki creators would have exactly 6000 years (10 NER: Great Years) until they themselves were dealt with (Armageddon). In Babylon, the hero was Marduk, a late post-flood invention. Marduk rode upon the back of a cherub in his fight against Tiamat [dragon of disaster].[18]

In Aegean astrology the Man [Bootes] and Woman [Virgo] descend over the western horizon [Fall of Mankind] as in the east the constellation Perseus rises, helm and armor with flaming sword, a being of vengeance.[19]

The Norse Eden was Muspelheim, guarded by the giant Surtur, who had a flaming sword with which he guarded a gate. It was this fiery sword

[Phoenix] that brought warmth to meet the frozen world of before.[20]

In Egypt, the winged disk exhibited two serpents and was a solar symbol of a "god of judgement" with power to separate good and evil.[21] Long ago in China, the dragon (serpent) was a symbol for "cataclysm." The tree was the symbol of "life."[22]

In the Gnostic texts, the serpent is the helper of Adam and Eve, who opens their eyes showing humans that their creator's *"...were beastly forms."*[23] He was, in Sumerian texts, called Enki, the only Anunnaki to show compassion to humans.[24] This traumatic event involving the serpent savior is the origin of the later traditions of serpent-like men who led survivors after a catastrophe, like Cecrops of Athens (see 1687 BCE).

Almost a thousand years ago the Jewish commentator Rashi wrote about the Great Deluge, which we clearly know occurred in 2239 BCE, and astonishingly, we find Rashi declaring that, *"...every 1656 years a similar disaster occurs."* This identifies 3895 BCE as a *"similar disaster"* like the Deluge, which almost totally depopulated the world. Scientists note that during the last ice age the Mediterranean was dry land.[25]

At depths of thousands of feet below the surface of the Pacific Ocean are peculiar, flat-topped mountains that could have only formed above sea level.[26]

The scientifically documented submarine topography of the Atlantic Ocean's mountain ranges, valleys, and other geological features are now known to have been *"...carved by agencies acting above the water level."*[27]

In polar Spitzbergen is found under the ice pack the frozen surface of a beach and successive layers of fossilized plants, tropical and equatorial. Wilkins wrote, *"It is difficult to suggest an explanation unless you visualize our earth tilted at the poles, under the impact of some body from outer space and slowly swinging through an arc of ninety degrees, so that equator and poles change place."*[28]

Our present equator was established in this year, changing from an older one in the month of May. Our present equator as we know it today was, before May of 3895 BCE, actually the north south axis.

That North America was formerly buried under glacial masses and uninhabited is supported by Lewis Spence – *"Not only does America furnish no tangible evidence of antiquity so great as to support the theory of an independent origin for American man, but… all American aboriginal culture is classed as Neolithic, and there appears to be no evidence of Paleolithic life."*[29]

In 3895 BCE is a lithospheric displacement, a shift of the crust of 30-45 degrees. The geographical distribution of the world's continental landmasses took on their present positions after the pole shift in May of this year. Prior to this date, the continents were much larger, oceans were smaller, and the north polar axis pointed at the star Alpha Draconis, the Eye of the Dragon.

3895 BCE is the third known global catastrophe:

1.   Nemesis Cataclysm, pre-5239 BCE
2.   Phoenix destruction of 4309 BCE
3.   3895 BCE pole shift.

The 4309 BCE Phoenix destruction ruined a thriving global civilization and scattered its survivors. The 3895 BCE pole shift was worse, and it BURIED THE EVIDENCE of this cataclysm beneath ice caps and oceans.

The pole shift event, altering the topography and the heavens as viewed by archaic people on earth, was widely regarded later as Year One of the 1656 years of the recorded Antediluvian World – or 1656 years of human history before the Great Deluge in May 2239 BCE. This 3895 BCE Year One was also the start of a 6000-year period to the prophesied formation of another New Heavens and New Earth to unfold in 2106 CE. Originally, the Creation Event was not a creation at all, but a renovation from the ruins of a prior world. But through time, the religious authorities have altered the truth of cataclysm causing the appearance of a new heavens and new earth in the distant past, and modelled their prophecies to fit this mold, thus claiming that at the end of this 6000-year period a New Heavens will appear for a New Earth… but this will be due to a vast and violent catastrophic destruction, just as it was in the past.

The displacement of the lithosphere was accompanied by the eruption of numerous volcanoes on land and undersea. As hundreds of magma domes blew open, volcanic ash thickened an already water-enriched atmosphere. Intense volcanism saturated the vapor canopy with ambient radiation (see 1902 CE for a modern example) that produced gigantism among the fauna and flora. This newly formed vapor canopy from 4039 BCE, and ambient radiation saturation of the animal and vegetable worlds, is the origin of the megafauna, the sudden appearance of gigantic mammalian and marsupial life forms in the archeological record. Prior to this cataclysm, the world was dominated by marsupials. This gigantism effect from ambient radiation was compounded by the greenhouse effect, resulting in a level of carbon monoxide much denser than today. This antediluvian atmosphere may have had as much as a thousand times more carbon dioxide as today. As plants thrive on carbon dioxide, the flora would have been lush and prolific.[30] Plants and animals would have grown to prodigious sizes, as plants steadily absorbed carbon monoxide-releasing oxygen in astounding quantities, inhaled by fauna of gigantic sizes, with all exhaling carbon monoxide in a feedback loop that kept the world at a tropical climate with minimal cooling at the poles.

Earth's vapor canopy (the biblical "firmament above) of water and carbon dioxide produced a daytime sky full of light, but with no visible Sun. The capture of long-wave radiation resulted in a greenhouse effect – diffusing light and warmth into the Polar Regions and creating a uniform temperature all year long. Summer and winter were not dissimilar and years were counted by stellar revolutions, with diurnal motion observed at night around the pole star Alpha Draconis. That Earth once had a vapor canopy like Venus has today, is a theory put forth by many, including Donald Patton in *The Biblical Flood and the Ice Epoch*.[31]

The megafauna pose yet another irritation to establishment historians. These enormous mammals were confidently assigned to an Ice Age period but it is now confidently concluded by meticulous analysis of preserved frozen mammoths, saber-tooth cats, woolly rhinosaurus, and other megafauna that these animals were NOT living in a frozen world but in a temperate-to-tropical environment when they were quick-frozen. That the Earth in times past was a glaciosphere of frozen wastes cannot be disputed, but the vast durations of Ice Ages are a complete fiction.

The rise of the megafauna coincided with the decline of the marsupials which died out mostly. Australia is an isolated fossil-continent survivor of this cataclysmic displacement. Thousands of varieties of marsupials from pre-mammalian antiquity are lost but some survive, and almost all of them in Australia – the kangaroo, kangaroo-rat, wallaby, platypus, the flying fox, the dingo, Tasmanian wolf, sloths, giant land birds (winged and wingless) like the emu, anteater (myrmecobius), wombat, flying phalanger, mole (Notoryctidae), native cat (dasyures), and mouse (dasycercus). The scientific names are provided because these are unique marsupials having mammalian (placentals) counterparts.

The emu and other giant land birds, marsupials and other peculiar fauna, all presently inhabiting the southern hemisphere, are the survivors of the pre-vapor canopy world. There were once massive land bridges connecting Australia, Madagascar, southern India, southern Africa and South America, to a tropical continent known to have existed from the numerous specimens of flora and fauna found under the Antarctic icepack.

Australia's great flightless bird, the emu, has its cousins only in the southern hemisphere (ancient pre-3895 BCE equatorial continent). The moa of New Zealand is one of the largest birds that ever existed, having no wings at all, a true biped, and its feathers are so primitive that they seem more like hairs. Some moas were 12 feet tall and they died out only very recently, within the last four centuries CE.[32] The kiwi of New Zealand has hairy feathers and vestiges of wings; it is the only bird in the world with its nostrils at the end of its beak.[33] As birds are DNA-modified lizards, the following fact concerning the New Zealand lizard tuatara is relevant. It is a unique lizard, the sole survivor of the order of rhynchocephalia, a lizard that antedates the dinosaurs. It is large, at over 2 feet in length, olive green, and has a vestige of a third eye atop its skull, the pineal eye.[34] This southern hemispheric ecology is truly archaic, home to the tassel fish, or, coelacanth, an index fossil creature believed extinct 65 million years ago until a local fisherman caught a living one off the coast of South Africa in 1938.

Primeval forms of marsupials once abounded in Europe but are no longer there. South America, India and Australia are rife with marsupials today, and among reptiles the same are found in Australia as in South America, and amphibian tree frogs of the same species are found only in Australia and Chili, South America.[35] Further, Professor Angelo Heilprin in 1887 wrote – *"The presence of lemurs on the island of Madagascar, the continent of Africa and southern India (with Ceylon), has led some naturalists to the conclusion that at one time direct land connection existed between the several regions."*[36] Lemurs are also on Australia. Lewis Spence also notes that the same species of freshwater fish are also distributed among these southern hemispheric regions.

Captain Cook sailed into Australian waters in 1770 CE, documenting enormous saltwater crocodiles, giant sharks, and huge ant and termite mounds the height of a man. In 1966, Alan Moorehead wrote of Cook's expedition, *"They soon became aware that they were confronted here with something infinitely strange: an utter primitivism, wild creatures that had not developed beyond the marsupial stage, plants that did not appear to fit into the Linnaean or indeed any other system of classification, a nomadic people [Aborigines] who lived more like animals than men. It was as though they were looking straight back into the beginnings of Creation."*[37] Australia was never developed by men long ago, a continent absolutely devoid of any technolithic, heliolithic or otherwise megalithic or any ancient architecture. And as all rules are defined by their exceptions, so too does the opossum stubbornly defy the marsupial dominance of the southern hemisphere. The opossum thrives in North America, the last vestige of marsupials outside the southern hemisphere.[38] It lives in North, Central and South America and NOWHERE in Europe, Asia or Africa.

Prior to the cataclysm we can see from the distribution of surviving species of marsupials today, that there had been a supercontinent – that Australia, New Zealand, Tasmania, Southern Africa, South America, and southern India had all been connected as ONE LANDMASS. Geologists have identified another landmass called the Miocene Bridge that merged the Americas to Europe and Asia. The pre-3895 BCE world had major marsupial and megafauna-occupied tropical landmasses where the North Atlantic Ocean and southern Pacific Antarctic oceans are located today. The megafauna survived the catastrophe but would, after 3895 BCE, gradually reduce in size closer to their present sizes. At this period in human history, Neanderthal survivors were feral predators and colonies of Cro-Magnon also persisted, some interbreeding with the Negroid, Mongolid, Amerindic and dark Caucasoid humans at various stages of Paleolithic, Mesolithic and Neolithic illiterate cultures. We know that humans hunted the megafauna because spear points, arrowheads, and cut bones of ancient camps tell the tales, however, there are NO TRADITIONS passed down from antiquity concerning the megafauna – no legends, no ancestral memories from any people in the world of animals being of such enormous sizes. This is simply because the megafauna diminished in size prior to the advent of literacy that exploded among the human population after 2239 BCE. The ambient radiation and vapor canopy world that caused the animals to grow to such enormous sizes ended with the Great Deluge cataclysm in 2239 BCE.

After the pole shift of 3895 BCE, the Mediterranean valley region was dry land and part of the Sahara desert of North Africa was a sea.

The entire Mediterranean basin was a vast, forested dry valley region.[39] Enki fathered civilized humans with experimentation and planning. But among the Anunnaki a controversy developed. A faction of the Anunna called the Igigi (Watchers) stationed offworld (Mars/Moon) revolted and descended to earth. They abducted human females and experimented with DNA, producing monsters, giants, hybrids and even heroes.

Humans were primitive workers, or, lulu.[40] This protohuman was manufactured using primate mammalian eggs infused with Anunna DNA, with many experiments having originally failed. In the ancient Sumerian, the original human creation was called lulu. Genesis 5:2 reads that God created man, male and female, and called their name Adam. However, the original Hebrew differs, and itself was a corruption of what the Jews found in the older Babylonian tablet writings from which they heavily borrowed when writing Genesis. The original Babylonian text conveyed that the gods created mankind male and female and called them the Adamu.

This lithospheric displacement (crustal shift) in 3895 BCE was an extinction level event for many species, involving intense volcanism that saturated the marine water canopy above with ambient radiation that produced gigantism among surviving fauna and flora. The megafauna – so well attested in worldwide archeological findings – are the remains of the Antediluvian World. During this unstable period volcanic resurfacing, quakes, upheavals and subsidence, and flooding produced over a dozen layers of strata, each a testament to the violence of the time. The Geologic Column hypothesis, holding that each deposit is hundreds of thousands to millions of years old, is in error. As will be shown, Homo sapiens remains have been found fossilized in strata concluded to be millions of years in age. Alluvial resurfacing has been observed in our lifetime to have produced more than one deposit from a single regional flooding. Establishment scientists, desperate to foist natural selection and evolutionary models over our concepts of the past, merely contribute to burying evidence of our cataclysmic history – they are loathe to admit that Charles Darwin himself was a catastrophist, who wrote in 1834, *"Certainly, no fact in the long history of the world is so startling as the wide and repeated exterminations of its inhabitants."*[41] Off the French Polynesian island of Rap Iti have been found undersea coal deposits, indicating that the Pacific basin was once dry land.[42]

1. Flying Serpents and Dragons p. 23; 2. Josephus, Jewish War on 70 AD 6.5.3., Pliny 2.22.89, 1 Chronicles 21:16, Revelation 1:16; 3. Gerald Massey Lectures p. 148; 4. Lost Language of Symbolism II p. 162; 5. Gerald Massey Lectures p. 183; 6. Lost Language of Symbolism II p. 276; 7. The Knights Templar in the New World p. 125; 8. The Rosicrucian Cosmo-Conception p. 500; 9. Sargon the Magnificent, p. 121 note 1; 10. Ezekiel 14:21-23; 11. St. Paul in Britain p. 12; 12. Book of the Damned p. 163; 13. Elder Gods of Antiquity p. 193; 14. Genesis Revisited p. 104; 15. Space Travelers and the Genesis of the Human Form p. 61; 16. Gods of Eden: Brambly, pgs. 38-49; 17. Space Travelers and the Genesis of the Human Form, p. 61; 18. Symbols, Sex and the Stars p. 61; 19. The Christ Conspiracy p. 189; 20. Lost Race of the Giants p. 75; 21. The Mammoth Book of Lost Symbols p. 105; 22. Secret Cities of Old South America p. 273; 23. Humanity's Extraterrestrial Origins p. 89; 24. ibid p. 98; 25. The Message of the Sphinx p. 21; 26. Lost Cities of Ancient Lemuria p. 208; 27. Atlantis: The Antediluvian World p. 40; 28. Mysteries of Ancient South America p. 21; 29. Atlantis in America: Spence p. 134; 30. Flying Serpents and Dragons p. 160; 31. Flying Serpents and Dragons p. 93; 32. Lost Cities of Ancient Lemuria and the Pacific p. 155; 33. Lost Cities of Ancient Lemuria and the Pacific p. 155; 34. Lost Cities of Ancient Lemuria and the Pacific p. 155; 35. Problem of Lemuria pgs. 166-168; 36. Problem of Lemuria pgs. 166-168; 37. The Fatal Impact p. 118; 38. Lost Cities of Ancient Lemuria and the Pacific p. 96; 39. Lost Cities of Atlantis, Ancient Europe…pgs. 204-205; 40. The Lost Book of Enki p. 126; 41. Atlantis in America: p. 69 citing Journal, 1834; 42. Lost Cities of Ancient Lemuria & the Pacific, p. 226.

3880 BCE (15 AM): 5985 Before Armageddon/ 1641 Before Flood/ 1359 Nemesis Cataclysm/ 429 Phoenix Year/ 159 Capture of Luna

According to the ancient Book of Jasher, Cain and Abel were twins, Cain slaying Abel when they were 15 years of age. This story immortalized the worldwide legends of the Twins always at war with one another. By this time, Chevah (Eve) had two or three more children, daughters. Abel was the firstborn and first murdered human, foreshadowing the atonement of the Messiah in the person of Christ, also called Shiloh. This was 3880 years to the start of the Anno Domini (Common Era) calendar (Year of the Lord) and the gematrical value for "Shiloh comes" is 3880.

3765 BCE (130 AM): 5870 Before Armageddon/ 1526 Before Flood/ 1474 Nemesis Cataclysm/ 544 Phoenix Year/ 274 Capture of Luna

As humankind rapidly multiplies, Seth is born, chosen by God to carry on the Messianic bloodline and be the future patriarch of the Sethites, who construct the Great Pyramid complex at Achuzan (Giza). Adam and Eve had many other children.[1]

1. *Antiquities of the Jews, 2:3:68.*

3761 BCE (134 AM): 5866 Before Armageddon/ 1522 Before Flood/ 1478 Nemesis Cataclysm/ 548 Phoenix Year/ 278 Capture of Luna/ 1 Jewish Calendar

The Jewish Calendar begins from *"...the years that have passed since the counting of years began."*[1]

This popularized beginning-date finds its origin in the Seder Olam Rabbah, or the *Book of the Order of the World*, compiled by Rabbi Halafta before 160 CE. This deliberate deception is admitted by Jewish commentators who claim the 2nd century CE falsification of the chronology was to prevent people from interpreting Daniel's 70 weeks concerning the coming of the Messiah (Daniel 9:25). The setting back by 134 years was an attempt to force an interpretation that Simon Bar Kochba in 135 CE was the fulfillment, not Jesus.[2]

1. *Flying Serpents and Dragons, p. 103;* 2. *The Annals of the World, p. 932 Appendix 6.*

<u>3760 BCE</u> (135 AM): **5865 Before Armageddon/ 1521 Before Flood**

Sitchin claims the beginning of mankind's calendar originated in Nippur (in Sumeria) 5800 years ago, and that it is still adhered to today by the Jews.[1] This date is completely impossible based on known records. Sitchin specifically dates the beginning of mankind's calendar not by any archeological discovery or *discovered* ancient calendar, but solely by the <u>Jewish Calendar</u> that today is descended from a system of chronology that was <u>altered</u> 2000 years ago by rabbinical Hebrews.

1. *When Time Began, p. 17.*

<u>3757 BCE</u> (138 AM): **5862 Before Armageddon/ 1518 Before Flood/ 1482 Nemesis Cataclysm/ 552 Phoenix Year/ 282 Capture of Luna**

Planet Phoenix passes through the inner solar system on its 138-year orbit of the Sun on its way back to the Kuiper Belt.

<u>3725 BCE</u> (170 AM): **5830 Before Armageddon/ 1486 Before Flood/ 1514 Nemesis Cataclysm/ 584 Phoenix Year/ 314 Capture of Luna**

At 40 years old, Seth begins ruling over the Adamites, establishing a kingdom. The early Egyptians venerated him as Set and only late in Egyptian antiquity, as newer gods came into vogue, was Set (Seth) demonized, falling into disrepute. The Sethite Kingdom and center of pre-Flood civilization was in Egypt.

<u>3700 BCE</u> (195 AM): **5805 Before Armageddon/ 1461 Before Flood/ 1539 Nemesis Cataclysm/ 609 Phoenix Year/ 339 Capture of Luna**

The archeological evidence appears to indicate that prior to about 3700 BCE there was no substantial culture to be found anywhere on the surface of the world.[1]

1. *Adam When? p. 80.*

<u>3619 BCE</u> (276 AM): **5724 Before Armageddon/ 1380 Before Flood/ 1620 Nemesis Cataclysm/ 690 Phoenix Year/ 420 Capture of Luna**

Planet Phoenix passes through the inner solar system on its 138-year orbit on its way back out to the Kuiper Belt.

3615 BCE (280 AM): 5720 Before Armageddon/ 1376 Before Flood/ 1624 Nemesis Cataclysm/ 694 Phoenix Year/ 424 Capture of Luna

Mankind begins falling away from the teaching of Seth and Adam, beginning to worship the creation rather than the Creator. This completes 7 generations, a generation being 40 years. Prior to this time, there was virtually no strife or crime and this period is remembered in the Japanese traditions known as The Way of the Gods. The account is recorded by Josephus in *Antiquities*.

3530 BCE (365 AM): 5635 Before Armageddon/ 1291 Before Flood/ 1709 Nemesis Cataclysm/ 779 Phoenix Year/ 509 Capture of Luna

Cainan, son of Enosh, begins ruling the Adamites at age 40, ending Seth's reign of 195 years. Cainan is wise and knowledgeable, famous for his power over spirits and demons. He was troubled by premonitions of a future disaster, the drowning of the entire world.[1]

1. Jasher 2:11.

3499 BCE (396 AM): 5604 Before Armageddon/ 1260 Before Flood/ 1740 Nemesis Cataclysm/ 810 Phoenix Year/ 540 Capture of Luna

The Nemesis X Object enters the inner solar system for the first time in human memory, emerging from southern space to begin its 60-year pass north of the ecliptic plane to finish its 792-year orbit. Nemesis X Object is <u>inhabited</u>.

3481 BCE (414 AM): 5586 Before Armageddon/ 1242 Before Flood/ 1758 Nemesis Cataclysm/ 828 Phoenix Year/ 558 Capture of Luna

Planet Phoenix passes through the inner solar system 18 years after Nemesis X Object passed over the ecliptic in the inner solar system. Both planets travel along the Dark Star's ecliptic between Venus and Earth. Phoenix continues on its 138-year orbit back into the Kuiper Belt. This is the 49th year of the reign of Cainan.

3468 BCE (427 AM):
Chinese traditional date of the birth of a prophet named Fuh-Ke who foretold of the coming of a Savior.[1] This anachronism may refer to Enoch who is born 195 years later.

1. *The Secret Doctrine, p. 68.*

3446 BCE (449 AM):
Extensive chronological calculations of a Leipzig theologian named Dr. Seyffarth, published in a book in 1900 CE, declared, *"uncontestably"* that the deluge ended at this date and the alphabets of the races of the world were invented.[1] This is seven years before the Flood of Enosh in 3439 BCE, and indeed, Enoch would soon invent a system of writing.

1. *Atlantis: the Eighth Continent, p. 14.*

3443 BCE (452 AM): 5548 Before Armageddon/ 1204 Before Flood/ 1796 Nemesis Cataclysm/ 866 Phoenix Year/ 596 Capture of Luna
David Davidson's calculation of 3443 is actually 4 years off from the correct year of 3439 BCE, but still remarkably close concerning Alpha Draconis being able to be sighted by an observer, looking up from the bottom of the Great Pyramid's Descending Passage at midnight of the autumnal equinox. This would have required two apertured diaphragms fixed into the passage.[1]

1. *The Great Pyramid: Its Divine Message.*

3439 BCE (456 AM): 5544 Before Armageddon/ 1200 Before Flood/ 1800 Nemesis Cataclysm/ 870 Phoenix Year/ 600 Capture of Luna
Nemesis X Object completes its 792-year orbit after passing for 60 years over the ecliptic, north of the Sun's position, and passes dangerously close to Earth. The Jasher records reads, *"And in the days of Enosh... the Lord caused the waters of the Gihon to overwhelm them, and He destroyed and consumed them, and He destroyed a third part of the earth... and there was no food for the sons of men and the famine was severe in those days."*[1] Hebrew tradition holds that there were many earthquakes, drought and famine in the days of Enosh[2] and in the Jewish

Haggadoth text we find that this flood in Enosh's day occurred before the famous Flood of Noah.[3] The Yezidis of Asia preserve traditions of a flooding more ancient than Noah's, stating that the world was flooded twice, the second flood by far the worse.[4]

Moses Maimonides wrote that in the days of Enosh men began to build temples to the host of heaven, venerating the stars as deities and the Old One, the Creator, over time, was forgotten.[5] The worship of the Anunnaki from the stars, called Watchers, is the theme of the older portions of the Book of Enoch. The Greeks remembered the Anunnaki as Annedoti, who were believed to have descended to Earth at 4 different times long ago interacting with men.[6] The Holy Tablets, fragments borrowed from Sumerian and Babylonian texts, indicate that the Anunnaki were imprisoned on the Nemesis X Object, but were able to get to Earth after a 60-year period.[7] In the Book of Enoch it was 200 Watchers that came down to Earth[8] and their leader, Azazel, was guilty of *"...disclosing to the world all the secret things which are done in the Heavens."*[9]

Zecharia Sitchin remarks in his *The Wars of Gods and Men* that Sumerian texts over and over refer to a starting point in the chronicles of the Anunnaki that began 432,000 *"years"* before the Deluge. Sitchin cites a text excavated from the ruins of Sumer concerning the descent of a god named EN.KI to Earth at that time which reads, *"When I approached Earth, there was much flooding..."*[10] Sitchin's research confirms this 3439 BCE date as the descent of the Anunnaki to Earth. In his *End of Days* book he relates that the Sumerian writings claim that the Anunnaki appeared on Earth when the Nemesis X Object orbited close to our planet 432,000 *"years"* before the Great Flood.[11] But this 432,000 years is a mistranslation commonly done with ancient Near East texts, for these are not 432,000 years, but 432,000 days. This equals precisely 1200 years of 360 days each, as seen in this chronology. As a result, the Great Flood date is fixed by the Phoenix orbit and is exactly 1200 years before this descent of the Anunnaki in 3439 BCE. In *Hamlet's Mill*, by Giorgio de Santillana and Hertha von Dechend, we see that the number 432,000 seems to be where science and myth merge, this number significant in the mythological systems around the world.[12]

The architecture of the Great Pyramid demonstrates this date of 3439 BCE. Astronomer Royal for Scotland, Charles Piazzi Smyth, in the 1870s during his research on site at the Great Pyramid, determined for unknown reasons that the descendant passage of the structure which goes all the way below the pyramid, pointed directly at Alpha Draconis (the Eye of the Dragon) in 3449 BCE, the pre-Flood pole star.[13] This is only a one year variance from 3439 BCE. This assessment was later reconfirmed by Davidson in his mammoth book in 1924 CE, *The Great Pyramid: Its Divine Message.*

The Anunnaki bound themselves with a mutual curse, accepting that they were adding more judgements upon themselves when they planned to teach mankind all the forbidden knowledge and sciences. When they appear among men they are rejected by the Sethite survivors but are taken in by the Canaanites, who give them their daughters in exchange for their aid and knowledge. The Watchers taught mankind herbalism, sorcery, incantations, power over evil spirits (ghosts of pre-Adamic people), and the Watchers fathered hybrids that grew to astonishing sizes, great giants called Nephilim. Mankind learned forbidden practices against animals, metallurgy, weaponsmithing, how to craft killing machines, the creation of jewelry and feminine cosmetics, stellar and lunar astronomy and astrology.[14] Their chief trespass was to teach humans how to brew spermicides.[15]

Men began to worship the stars and the Eternal One gave them what they wanted. The Anunnaki descended and men began to worship them as gods. A third of humanity was killed in the disasters caused by Nemesis X Objects' pass in 3439 BCE, and a third of humanity will likewise perish in 2046 CE when the Nemesis X Object initiates the Trumpet Judgements of Revelation in the Apocalypse, when a third of mankind dies.

Charles Fort in 1919 CE wrote, *"There may have been a lost colony or lost expedition from somewhere, upon this earth, and extra-mundane visitors who never could get back, there have been other extra-mundane visitors, who have gone away again…"*[16]

Erich Von Däniken's interpretation, *"Enoch's Angels were mutineers against the Lord. A considerate team of 200 members rebelled against their commander, who, as Enoch knew, finally vanished into Space in a spaceship and left the mutineers behind on the earth."*[17]

(*Chronotecture*). Descent of the Watchers 534 years to 2905 BCE, began building the Great Pyramid.

Enoch as a man is a Jewish Fiction. He is none other than the Anunna person named Enki, his full Sumerian title being Enmeduranki ((en) meduran(ki). It was Enki who built the Great Pyramid.

Oannes was the first of the Apkallu, the Seven Demigods of ancient Sumer. They served as counselors and priests to the kings of Sumer before the flood.[18]

Enki protested the use of forbidden weapons on earth.[19]

Writing began right after this date, pictographic, hieroglyphic, and cuneiform.

The first skeletal remains of dogs were found in Iran, Iraq and Israel.[20]

Sitchin notes that the ancient Egyptians preserved a memory of a very Great God who visited in the earliest times at a time of bad flooding, when he undertook great works of reclamation. Sitchin asserts this was ENKI, building dams, canals, and irrigation works along the Nile in Egypt.[21] He connects a Sumerian God to earliest Egypt. This would be 3439 BCE. Sitchin also connects this memory to the idea that ancient Egyptians called Egypt The Raised Land, which is wrong. An event in 1899 BCE, 1540 years later, is why Egypt came to be called the Raised Land.

Oannes was one of Seven Anunnaki that emerged from the sea.[22]

Enki arrived strictly to mine metals.[23]

Thor Heyerdahl remarks, *"The real puzzle was that human history has no known beginning. As it stands, it begins with civilized mariners coming in by sea. This is no real beginning. This is the continuation of something lost somewhere in the mist."*[24]

Astronomer Royal for Scotland, Piazzi Smyth, noted that the scored line in the Descendant Passage of the monument pointed directly at Alpha Draconis in the year 3440 BCE (his approximate), which is a one year variance from the actual date of 3439 BCE. Alpha Draconis was the Eye of the Dragon and the Anunnaki were the Watchers, a word in Semitic derived from ancient roots meaning dragon and seeing.

Berossus wrote that when Oannes appeared, humans were like *"...the beasts of the field."*[25]

3439 BCE is the original descent of the Anunnaki and numbered 50 individuals.[26]

Mixtec tradition of Southwest Mexico states, *"In the days of obscurity and darkness* [during the time of the vapor canopy, before the Sun was 'born' in the 2239 BCE Great Flood] *when there were as yet no days nor years, the world was a chaos sunk in darkness, while the earth was covered with water, on which slime and scum floated. One day the Deer God and Goddess appeared. They had human form, and out of their magic* [technology] *they raised a great mountain out of the* water [Giza complex pyramids/temples] *and built on it beautiful palaces for their dwelling... the mountain* [pyramid] *which was called Place Where the Heavens Stood... the Deer Gods had more sons and daughters, but there came a Flood* [2239 BCE] *in which many of these perished."*[27] The Children of the Gods built a garden of their own but it was destroyed in the Flood, killing many *"...sons and daughters of the gods."*[28]

Erudu was not in Sumer or Babylonia. Enki's city was Giza, in Egypt, preserved in Enki's son's name – NIN'GISH'ZIDDA.

The Holy Tablets are a collection of Babylonian, Akkadian, Assyrian, and cuneiform fragments, some being copies of older Sumerian texts, that indicate that the Anunnaki are contained on Nemesis X Object, but have a 60-year window when they can come to earth.[29]

The pre-Sumerian period was the Ubaid, possibly dating as early as 3700 BCE, two or three centuries before 3439 BCE when the Anunna arrived. Amidst its history, a major flooding occurred that deposited a thick layer of clean, water-laid silt discovered in multiple excavation sites in 1929 CE -1934 CE by Sir Leonard Wooley. Ubaid remains and artifacts were found below and above the flood stratum, exhibiting the continuity of this culture.[30] It is only after this flood deposit that major developments occur. Virtually overnight, the primitive Ubaid culture suddenly underwent a transition into a populous civilization of agriculturalists and builders from small communities of hunter-gatherer fisherman. Anthropologists theorize that rapid changes in primitive culture to such advancements are evidence of new contact with a higher civilization; introduced material.

Sir Leonard Wooley discovered among Ubaid artifacts long-skulled statues of a serpent like people, even serpentine infants, males and females.[31] This tradition of serpent gods was anterior to the arrival of the Anunna, who were originally depicted as tall, bearded Caucasians visiting a world of black-eyed, black-haired short humans, smooth-skinned humans.

Apollodorus also studied the now lost records of Berossus. He criticized Abydenus (later 4th century BCE) for not mentioning the other amphibious beings who arrived with Oannes. Collectively called the Annedoti, semi-demons described as *repulsive abominations.*[32] Robert Temple wrote, *"...if ever anything argued the authenticity of their account, it was this Babylonian tradition that the amphibians to whom they owed everything were disgusting, horrible and loathsome to look upon."*[33] Another of the Annedoti was Odacon, later to be known throughout the post-Diluvian Near East as Dagon.[34]

There are no Sumerian records of any flying machines, spacecraft, space flight, no floating buildings nor are there any relics of technolithic architecture as found at Giza, Puma Punku and a few other sites. That there exist two different versions of the appearance of the Anunnaki is because one is true and the other fictive; the appearance of Enki and others was by ship from the sea [Deep]. Later, as the Anunnaki were regarded as deities, it was told they had come from the heavens [where gods dwell].

The Nile River was called the Geion [Gihon] by the Coptic Christians of Egypt.[35]

Prior to the arrival of Enki, humans were primitive hunter-gatherers.

3439 BCE, Year 1 Contact Period, is 792 years to 2647 BCE, the arrival of Anunna to their Exodus.

3439 BCE is 1540 years to 1899 BCE, when humans are attacked by the Anunna.

EA [Enki] pilots a ship to earth containing 50 Anunnaki heroes.[36] EA is the origin of later Babylonian Oannes. EA means *He Whose Home is Water.*[37] EA's official title among the Anunna was ENKI [Lord of the Earth]. He was the firstborn of ANU. He was from offworld and later remembered as the extraordinary person of Enoch.

Berossus accessed the ancient tablet texts of Harran.[38] This is in southeastern Turkey.

Enki's Adamu were black-haired, smooth-skinned and dark red, according to Zecharia Sitchin.[39] They could not produce and were made to be laborers. Enki's genetic material was planted in Anunnaki female carriers [birth-goddesses].[40] But the production of workers was too slow, so Enki manufactured lulu females to accompany the Adamu. But it still took invitro-fertilization of Anunnaki-females to produce humans that could procreate on their own.

Sitchin notes that Anunna-human interbreeding was carried on by Enki and his sanctioned group, and by the unsanctioned criminal element known as the Igigi, the Watchers.[41]

Anunna brought livestock from their world to earth. They also brought cereals, the first grains. The existence of the cow is an anomaly. Such a defenseless, weak and slow creature would never had survived natural selection. The evolutionary model fails to account for the cow. The bovine could never have lived and evolved over eons with the world full of so many predatory species. The bovine owes his existence to a protective agency – humans.

Civilized man learned husbandry, agriculture, and became shepherds. As farmers, they were the opposite of the hunter-gatherers who were nomads.

Cotton plants are found growing in many parts of America in the wild, but never in the Old World. Cotton grown in the Americas is superior to that of the India cotton of Asia and when American cotton is taken to India, it grows into a poorer quality. Thus, it becomes evidence that cotton is native to America.[42]

The cotton gin was known in ancient Bronze Age China, as well as tobacco, potato, maize, white and yellow corn, and other plants believed to be indigenous to America.[43]

Wheat, oats, barley, rye, maize – the cereals were all brought to earth by Homo Anunna. This answers Ignatius Donnelley's question, *"Why is it that the origin [of these cereals] is totally lost in the mists of a vast antiquity?"*[44]

Ignatius Donnelly, concerning the traditions of Oannes, wrote, *"This is clearly the tradition preserved by a barbarous people of the great ships of a civilized nation, who colonized their coast and introduced the arts and sciences among them."*[45]

The Gihon River is identified by Flavius Josephus as the Nile River in Egypt.[46]

Oannes created man according to the Babylonians.[47] This identifies him as Anunnaki. He is also the father of metallurgy, a very unusual fact since no metals of any significance have ever existed in Mesopotamia.[48]

Arthur Mitchell wrote, *"There is a considerable leap from stone to bronze, but the leap from bronze to iron is comparatively small... it seems highly improbable, if not altogether absurd, that the human mind, at some particular stage of its development, should here, there, and everywhere – independently, and as the result of reaching that stage – discover that an alloy of copper and tin yields a hard metal useful in the manufacture of tools and weapons. There is nothing analogous to such an occurrence in the known history of human progress."[49]* Better put, Mitchell is here bearing light on the impossibility of civilizations everywhere, at the same time in the mid-fourth millennium BCE, of discovering alloys. The inference here is that this science was introduced by an unknown element.

Lenormant documented the discovery of bronze artifacts excavated near Memphis, Egypt from as early as the 4th millennium BCE.[50]

The alien-reptoid school is supported by traditional evidence, a few ancient sources, some archaic statuary, but little else. That the ancients believed their gods were reptilian only concerns a very small group. What is consistently ignored is that the earliest Sumerian reliefs, statuary, and seals show the Anunna over and over again as tall, bearded humans.

The Chinese maintain that an amphibious being with a man's head and fish's tail named Fuxi [Fu-Hsi] founded their civilization. The traditional Chinese date is 3322 BCE.[51] This is close to the truth, being 117 years after the arrival of Fuxi in 3439 BCE, and 1083 years before the Great Flood in 2239 BCE. Fuxi was the Celestial Emperor before the founding of the First Chinese Dynasty almost 12 centuries before the Hsia Dynasty [the 1st] began in 2205 BCE,[52] or 34 years after the Cataclysm.

Fuxi and his consort named Nu Gua (Nu Wa) repaired the heavens after a flood (Gihon Flood 3439 BCE Nile River). As civilization builders, they are often depicted holding a square and compass. Fuxi measured the earth and heavens by degrees and invented the calendar.[53] His wife Nu Gua was depicted as having a serpent's body. Fuxi is sometimes confused with Yu, the survivors of the Great Flood much later. As *Fu-hi*, he was said to have come down from on high and his primary concern was to measure *"...the dimensions of the world from east to west and north to south."*[54]

3439 BCE was the Technolithic Period/Age of Homo Anunna, 792 years to 2647 BCE Exodus.

Ignatius Donnelly said, *"The abyss between the civilized man and the savage is simply incalculable; it represents not alone a difference in arts and methods of life, but in the mental constitution, the instincts, and the predispositions of the soul... the one belongs to a building and creating race, the other to a wild, hunting stock. This abyss between savagery and civilization has never been passed by any nation through its own original force, and without external influences, during the historical period."*[55]

Rh-negative blood type is an introduction from an outside source, not naturally occurring in the human family. Many Rh-negative infants are born with a tail, a nerve-bundle surgically removed at birth.[56]

After the Flood of Gihon, the Homo Anunna appeared. The underlying message of Sumerian fragments concerning the Anunna was of their association with other planetary bodies, the Sun and the moon. But evidence of an extraterrestrial origin is lacking. Homo Anunna could have been on or under the earth all along, somewhere unknown, appearing from the sea in ships because their own homelands were destroyed. The later Babylonian deities that were called the Anunnaki were memories of pre-Cataclysm Homo Anunna, and the traditions from a direct origin from the stars were *not* of Homo Anunna, but belonged to Homo Anunna as their own beliefs of extraterrestrial parentage. It has been well documented over the centuries that in thousands of years of recorded invasions, migrations, and takeovers, the beliefs of the conquerors became the beliefs of the conquered.

"When a halo surrounds the Moon and Nibiru stands within it, there will be a slaughter of cattle and beasts of the field."[57] Note: The translator thought Nibiru (Nemesis X Object) might be a reference to Jupiter.

A planetary object called Marduk, at its appearance, is called Umunpauddu but after it has arisen for three hours or so, it then called Sagmigar but once it reaches the meridian of the sky, it becomes Nemesis X Object.[58] In 1900 CE, in the translations of Thomas Campbell of the old Akkadian and Babylonian texts, the scholars of the day arbitrarily inserted *Jupiter* in their translations, admitting that Jupiter was known by other names. But in their explanatory notes they concede that the actual three thousand year-old texts read **Nibiru** and Sagmigar, which was also Nibiru according to the ancient and modern translator.[59] Here is the text with Nibiru where it belongs, instead of using the interpolated Jupiter references – *"When Nibiru grows bright, the king of Akkad will go to pre-eminence. When Nibiru grows bright, there will be foods and rains... When Nibiru culminates, the gods will give peace, troubles will be cleared up, and complications will be unraveled. Rains and foods will come; the amount of crops with regard to the cold, will be out of all proportions to the amount of cold on the crops. The lands will dwell securely. Hostile kings will be at peace... From Nirgal-itir."*[60] This is clearly a *prophecy* of a future time of peace and prosperity caused by the appearance of Nemesis X Object. Nor is this the only reference to the appearance of Nemesis X Object bringing plenty and peace.[61] Scholars debated over the identity of this Nemesis X Object long before the birth of Zecharia Sitchin, who popularized it.

1. Jasher 2:3-7; 2. Flying Serpents and Dragons p. 132; 3. Ancient Egypt Light of the World Vol. II, p.567; 4. From the Ashes of Angels p. 183; 5. Morals and Dogma p. 327; 6. Return of the Serpents of Wisdom p. 44; 7. The Holy Tablets 1:47-48, p. 143 col. 1; 8. Book of Enoch 7:5-11; 9. Enoch 9:5; 10. The Wars of Gods and Men. p. 11. Sitchin, The End of Days 3; 12. When Time Began 10-11; 13. The Great Pyramid: Smyth 370; 14. Jasher 2:5-6, Enoch 7:6-15, 8:1-9; 15. Jasher 2:19-20; 16. Book of the Damned p. 159; 17. Pathway to the Gods p. 165; 18. The Ancient Alien Question 198; 19. The Lost Book of Enki p. 8; 20. The 12th Planet p. 9; 21. The 12ʰ Planet p. 418; 22. The Babylonian Theodicy p. 142; 23. The Wars of Gods and Men p. 80; 24. The Tigris Expedition p. 5; 25. The Rise and Fall of the Nephilim p. 99; 26. Divine Encounters p. 8; 27. The History of Atlantis: Spence p. 153-154; 28. Atlantis: The Antediluvian World: p. 270; 29. The Holy Tablets 1:47-48, p. 143 col. 1; 30. From the Ashes of Angels, p. 303; 31. From the Ashes of Angels p. 258-261; 32. The Sirius Mystery p. 277-278; 33. ibid 278; 34. ibid 276; 35. Gobekli Tepe: Genesis of the Gods: Andrew Collins p. 230; 36. The Lost Book of Enki p. 62; 37. Ibid, p. 6; 38. The Lost Book of Enki p. 4; 39. Lost Book of Enki p. 139; 40. ibid. p. 140-141; 41. ibid p. 264; 42. Atlantis: The Antediluvian World 48; 43. ibid p. 48-49; 44. Atlantis: The Antediluvian World p. 138; 45. Atlantis: The Antediluvian World p. 163; 46. Atlantis: The Antediluvian World p. 269; 47. The Sirius Mystery p. 167; 48. Atlantis in America p. 168; 49. Atlantis: The Antediluvian World p. 293; 50. Atlantis: The Antediluvian World p. 296; 51. The Sirius Mystery p. 289; 52. The Sirius Mystery p. 291; 53. The Sirius Mystery p. 290; 54. The Sirius Mystery p. 292; 55. Atlantis: The Antediluvian World p. 110; 56. Our Occulted History p. 240; 57. The Reports of the Magicians and Astrologers, p. lii.; 58. The Reports of the Magicians and Astrologers p. lii; 59. The Reports of the Magicians and Astrologers p. lxvi; 60. The Reports of the Magicians and Astrologers p. lxvi; 61. Ibid p. lxvi, No. 187.

3435 BCE (460 AM): 5540 Before Armageddon/ 1196 Before
     Flood/ 1804 Nemesis Cataclysm/ 874 Phoenix Year/ 604
     Capture of Luna/ 4 Anunna Arrival

The pre-Flood Patriarch Jared is born in this year, a holy man of the
Sethite lineage who was specifically named in commemoration of the
event of the descent of the Watchers from heaven.[1] His name is from
the root *ared*, to descend. He is a priest and will father the famous
Enoch, who will last be seen among men, ascending into heaven.

    1. Book of Jubilees 4:15.

3395 BCE (500 AM): 5500 Before Armageddon/ 1156 Before
     Flood/ 1844 Nemesis Cataclysm/ 914 Phoenix Year/ 644
     Capture of Luna/ 44 Anunna Arrival

Jared is 40 years old and distressed over the decadent social conditions
after observing how men and women had fallen prey to the Watchers.
Jared is shown a vision of God's appearance to Earth in the Last Days
and he is specifically told that His appearance among men will be in
5500 years.[1] This aligns perfectly with the Annus Mundi dating, for this
year is 500 AM, and 5500 years would place the return of God to Earth
in 2106 CE, the year 6000 Annus Mundi.

    1. Book of Adam and Eve II: 19:1, 20:15.

3375 BCE (520 AM): 5480 Before Armageddon/ 1136 Before
     Flood/ 1864 Nemesis Cataclysm

The beginning of the current Great Cycle of the Maya, as calculated
(4 ahau, 8 Cumnu) in 1950 CE by Ignatius Donnelly. But this is in
error due to 713 BCE alteration of the solar orbit duration from 360 to
365.25 days a year/cycle.

3373 BCE (522 AM): 5478 Before Armageddon/ 1134 Before
     Flood/ 1866 Nemesis Cataclysm/ 936 Phoenix Year/ 666
     Capture of Luna/ 66 Anunna Arrival/ 1 Olmec Calendar

This is the start-date of the ancient American Olmec Calendar as
discovered by Dr. H. J. Spinden of Harvard in several architectural
measurements of ruins in Central America, belonging to the Maya and
earlier Olmecs. 3373 BCE marks the beginning of their reckoning of
time.[1] This date is astronomically aligned with two prior significant

events. The Olmecs and Maya both reckoned their calendars in multiples of cycles involving 52-year periods. This date is 936 years after the world was destroyed and frozen solid in 4309 BCE, or 52x18 years, which began the Phoenix Year timeline. After Earth drifted for 270 years through space, it began to orbit the present Sun in 4039 BCE, or 666 years earlier. A third astronomical link is found in that the Olmec start-date was 66 years after Nemesis X Object passed and the Watchers descended to Earth – Nemesis X Object's orbit being 792 years, and 66 years is 792 months.

1. *Sargon the Magnificent p. 164; Flying Serpents and Dragons, p. 103.*

3361 BCE (534 AM): 5466 Before Armageddon/ 1122 Before Flood/ 1878 Nemesis Cataclysm/ 948 Phoenix Year/ 678 Capture of Luna/ 400 Jewish Calendar/ 12 Olmec Calendar

A strewn field of rock and ice fragments with a dust cloud having broken free of Nemesis X Object now enters the inner solar system as the *Ancient Earth-Killer* Comet Group. This mass of debris will assume a solar orbit exactly half of Nemesis X Object's 792 years, orbiting the Sun every 396 years. This year, of 3361 BCE, parallels the entire 3361 Pyramid Inch length of the Great Pyramid's Ascendant Passage, and the 534 Annus Mundi year here parallels the 534-inch length of the Kings Chamber floor at the Great Step at the top of the Ascendant Passage.

3359 BCE (536 AM):

Anu descended to earth to oversee Enki's mining operations. Sitchin notes that Enki's Anunnaki had been mining for 28,800 years, a ridiculous notion due to Sitchin's continued adherence to a fallacy – that the sums in Sumerian texts were of years. The proven fact is that they were *days*, not years. This 28,800 comes to 80 years (28,000 ÷ 360 days = 80 years) and 80 years after Enki's descent in 3439 BCE was Anu and Enlil's descent in 3359 BCE. Enlil was given command of the operation and such is probably the origin of Enki and Enlil's contention.[1] The decision to elevate Enlil over Enki is noted by Sitchin to derive from the fact that though Enki was firstborn of Anu, he was born of a concubine – while Enlil was later born of Anu's half-sister wife. Enlil was the robber of Enki's birthright.[2] Sitchin correctly observes that Anunnaki considerations of succession were predicated upon genetic purity.[3] The most acceptable Anunnaki unions involved coupling or marrying one's half-sister.[4] Thus, to the Anunnaki, the ultimate trespass was interracial coupling.

According to Sitchin, the 300 Igigi ("Those Who See and Observe") remained in constant orbit around the earth[5] as Watchers, of sorts, and being conduits in the transport of mined ores from the planet. The Igigi became involved in an uprising.

Under Enlil the Anunnaki themselves mined the ores, suffering, for *"...forty counted periods."*[7] Sitchin finds nowhere any reference to NIBIRU, or 40 NIBIRU orbits. His claim that the Anunnaki mined for 144,000 years is preposterous, which he simply derived by multiplying 3600x40. The Sumerian text reads 40 counted periods. This is important. Enki led the mining operations for 80 years (3429-3359 BCE) and Enlil took over for 40 years (3359-3319 BCE) to produce a total of 120 years, or the Sumerian shar, before the Anunnaki rebelled. The Anunnaki history from their descent to the Great Flood in 2239 BCE was ten shars, or ten periods of 120 years. At the end of the very first 120 year period of the Anunnaki on earth, they rebelled in 3319 BCE, 1080 years before the Great Deluge (2239 BCE).

1. The Wars of Gods and Men p. 80; 2. Ibid p. 81; 3. Ibid p. 81; 4. Ibid p. 82; 5. Ibid p. 87; 6. Ibid p. 91; 7. Ibid p. 102-103.

3343 BCE (552 AM): 5448 Before Armageddon/ 1104 Before Flood/ 1896 Nemesis Cataclysm/ 966 Phoenix Year/ 696 Capture of Luna/ 96 Anunna Arrival/ 30 Olmec Calendar

Planet Phoenix passes through the inner solar system, completing its 138-year orbit on its way back to the Kuiper Belt. As this is 552 Annus Mundi, this completes the first Phoenix Cycle since mankind was banished in 3895 BCE. Further, many connections between the planet Phoenix and the geometry of the Great Pyramid are seen throughout this research. In this year, which is 5448 years before Armageddon, Phoenix was probably clearly visible as this sum, 5448, is the precise Pyramid Inch height of the Great Pyramid without its capstone, a piece of architecture that fits atop the monument. It is symbolic of the return of the Chief Cornerstone that the Builders (Anunnaki) rejected, at Armageddon in 2106 CE.

3322 BCE (573 AM):
The traditional founding of Chinese civilization by semi-divine amphibious beings who also invented the calendar.[1]

1. *The Sirius Mystery, p. 289.*

3319 BCE (576 AM): 1080 Before Flood/ 120 Anunna Arrival
In the 120th year of their mining labors on earth, 80 years under Enki (3439-3359 BCE), and 40 years under Enlil (3359-3319 BCE), the Anunnaki rebelled, stopped laboring, rioted and sought to kill Enlil.[1] This was 414 years (138x3: Phoenix) before beginning of the Great Pyramid at Giza construction, 1080 years before the Great Flood (2239 BCE). Note: The Great Pyramid was completed in 2815 BCE, or year 1080 AM.
The holographic reflection of 3319 BCE is 9133, and 9133-3319 is 5814… the Great Pyramid being 5814 pyramid inches high.

1. *The Wars of Gods and Men, p. 109.*

3273 BCE (622 AM): 5378 Before Armageddon/ 1034 Before Flood/ 1966 Nemesis Cataclysm/ 1036 Phoenix Year/ 766 Capture of Luna/ 100 Olmec Calendar
Jared fathers Enoch, the seventh descendant from Adam in the Sethite line.[1] Enoch will emerge to be the most famous of all Antediluvian personages, remembered by ancient cultures around the world. At this time the Anunnaki are raising many sons, known as the Nephilim, sourced from Canaanites who continue to trade their daughters for Anunnaki knowledge and technology. These unions produced a race of giants and already, 166 years after the Descent of the Watchers, the Nephilim are becoming populous.

1. *Genesis 5:18.*

3233 BCE (662 AM): 5338 Before Armageddon/ 994 Before Flood/ 2006 Nemesis Cataclysm/ 1076 Phoenix Year/ 806 Capture of Luna/ 206 Anunna Arrival/ 140 Olmec Calendar
At age 40 Enoch begins his ministry and prophesies against the Nephilim and their Anunnaki fathers. He condemns the Canaanites who now live in total vice, practicing exogamy with the Nephilim

families and sharing their culture corrupted by intoxicants and hedonism.[1] Enoch is shown the Tables of Heaven, called Tablets of Destinies by the Sumerians, divine inscriptions of the past, present, and future histories of the Earth and the heavens.[2] He prophesied that the offspring of the angels, the giants, would perish off the face of the Earth and that only a handful of men would survive a terrible Flood. He foretold that even after this disaster the giants would reappear.[3] Enoch is made to comprehend the motion of the celestial bodies, the patterns of the stars and the constellations that are a luminous prophetic code interpreted and understood by the angels.[4] Enoch is taught by God the secrets of time and calendars[5] and is given divine instructions and plans on the building of a monument on earth that would serve as an enduring testimony to all future generations of Man. He is shown this monument and in a vision he sees *"...a great and lofty mountain, a strong rock... internally it was deep...and very smooth; as smooth as if it had been rolled over."*[6] The imagery here is of the Great Pyramid's smooth white limestone casing blocks as had faced the monument long ago, prior to 1356 CE, when an earthquake damaged the structure and locals mined the valuable stone for building material in Lower Egypt. Enoch is told by an angel that this structure is where the spirits of the righteous are collected.[7] This identifies it as the Altar of God as seen in Revelation, when during the Apocalypse the souls of the unjustly slain cry out to God for vengeance. As will be reviewed, the Great Pyramid is called *"the altar of God in the land of Egypt."*

Though Enoch was a pre-Flood prophet, the majority of his recorded prophecies concern the Last Days[8] when, according to him, the Watchers will again descend to earth to plague mankind. He claimed that the sons of the Watchers (giants, hybrid Nephilim offspring) will bear a terrible curse, for they were a hybrid abomination between angel and human. After God destroyed their bodies in a Flood, their spirits would roam the Earth as restless ghosts, evil spirits that corrupt, oppress, deceive (masquerading as trolls, imps, elves, and now aliens), contending with men and afflicting them as Phantoms, Specters, and Baleful Entities disguised as the souls of the dead people passed on.[9]

---

1. Tales of the Prophets, p. 88; 2. Enoch 92:1-20; 3. Enoch 105:14-16; 4. Enoch 105:23; 5. Jubilees 4:16-25; 6. Enoch 22:1-4; 7. Enoch 22:1-5; 8. Enoch 1:1-2; 9. Enoch 15:8-10

3208 BCE (687 AM): 5313 Before Armageddon/ 969 Before Flood/ 2031 Nemesis Cataclysm/ 1101 Phoenix Year/ 831 Capture of Luna

At 65 years of age, the prophet Enoch is made king of the Sethite line, a reign that will last 108,000 days (300 years of 360 days each). He fathers Methuselah, who will go on to live longer than any human has ever, or will ever, live during the period of banishment, an age of 969 years. Methuselah's name itself was actually a prophecy, meaning, *"when I die it [the Flood] shall come."* In fact, The Flood occurred in the same year Methuselah died, in 2239 BCE. The center of Sethite civilization before the Flood and the seat of Enoch's kingdom was in the geographical area known later as Egypt. Details on Enoch's kingship and Methuselah's birth in Genesis 5:21 and Jasher 3:12.

3205 BCE (690 AM): 5310 Before Armageddon/ 966 Before Flood/ 2034 Nemesis Cataclysm/ 1104 Phoenix Year/ 834 Capture of Luna/ 168 Olmec Calendar

In the 3rd year of Enoch's reign, planet Phoenix passed through the inner solar system, completing its 138-year orbit on its way back out to the Kuiper Belt. This completes the 2nd 552-year Phoenix Cycle from the start of the Phoenix Year cataclysm in 4309 BCE. As shown in *When the Sun Darkens*, the prophet Enoch is associated with legends of the Phoenix. As Phoenix is the planet of chronology, we are not surprised to find that Enoch is the most famous chronologist in antiquity.

3200 BCE (695 AM):

By this date the early Bronze Age was in full progress.[1]

1. *Elder Gods of Antiquity*, p. 210.

3195 BCE (700 AM): 5300 Before Armageddon/ 956 Before Flood/ 2044 Nemesis Cataclysm/ 1114 Phoenix Year/ 844 Capture of Luna

In this year, according to the *Apocalypse of Adam* found among the Gnostic *Nag Hammadi* texts of Egypt, Adam revealed to his son Seth the hidden knowledge of God concerning the destruction of the entire world by floodwaters as an act of the Wrath of God. Seth was told that there would be righteous survivors.[1] Seth was 570 years old at this time, and as will be shown, would be the principal architect of the Great Pyramid after Enoch's disappearance. Interestingly, this is 230 years before Adam's death in 2965 BCE, and 230 years is 2760 months, or 552x5. This was the 13th year of Enoch's reign.

1. *The Nag Hammadi Library, pgs. 279-280, 286.*

3175 BCE (720 AM):
3172 BCE, Sitchin cites conclusions of Maria Scholten de D'Ebneth, who published evidence that ancient South American ruins like Cuzco, Machu Picchu, Quito in Ecuador, Ollantaytambo, and Tiahuanacu were all part of a grid pattern that, when measured against the earth's obliquity (tilt), revealed that the grid was established at or about 3172 BCE.[1]

1. *The Lost Realms, p. 203-205.*

3165 BCE (730 AM): 5270 Before Armageddon/ 926 Before Flood/ 2074 Nemesis Cataclysm/ 1144 Phoenix Year/ 874 Capture of Luna/ 208 Olmec Calendar
Cain is killed in his old age by accident by a relative named Lamech. Philo wrote that Cain lived for 730 years.[1] This is 52x4 (208 years) of the Olmec Calendar.

1. *Sargon the Magnificent, p. 32.*

3163 BCE (732 AM): 5268 Before Armageddon/ 924 Before Flood/ 2076 Nemesis Cataclysm/ 1146 Phoenix Year/ 876 Capture of Luna/ 276 Anunna Arrival/ 210 Olmec Calendar
In the 45th year of the reign of Enoch, the Sethites erect several megalithic sites in the Northern Hemisphere after journeying from their homelands. The Carnac site in France is erected with multiple rows of megaliths as a calendar embodying the concept of a 360-day year.[1] Newgrange is built in Ireland, a gigantic earthworks having geometric alignments and parallels with Stonehenge in England. By the vernal equinox, Newgrange is finished. Astrophysicist Tom Ray of Dublin Institute for Advanced Studies discovered that sunlight would have penetrated the back wall of Newgrange's deep tunnel and chamber 5150 years back from when he calculated, at the exact moment the Sun emerged over the

eastern horizon. This date indicated 732 AM (3163 BCE). The builders then move to southern England and erect Stonehenge, which consists of an outer earthworks ring, which encircles a massive megalithic sarsen circle composed of huge lintels, averaging 25 tons each, that fit perfectly together in tongue-in-groove fashion, and with a curvature forming a perfect 360° circle. A number of bluestones were added later, in 3113 BCE (despite modern claims). The stunning chronometry of Stonehenge matches that of the Great Pyramid and is the subject of chapters in *Anunnaki Homeworld*. The great Trilithon at the center of the formation, the highest of the megaliths, is three gigantic blocks with 6 planes each, thus 6x6x6. This cube of six forms the gematria for DBIR, or Most Holy Place, which represents that a stone (symbol for man) contains something of importance to the Creator.[2] This is Enoch's 70th year of ministry against the Anunnaki and Nephilim.

Chapter 34 of Enoch is about Stonehenge, which reads, *"Towards the north to the ends of the earth, and I saw there a glorious device."* In the same area of Wales where the bluestones originated is a place that was long ago called Carn Enoch, and is still called that today. Further, the earliest name for the country around Newgrange in Ireland was Uriel, which happens to be the name of the angel in the Enochian writings that instructed the pre-Flood prophet.3 Stonehenge long ago was associated with Saturn, who was also known as Cronus (Time). [Sat] urn was originally Set[h], who was 602 years old in this year, with still more life to live. Seth would die during the 90 years of construction on the Great Pyramid. In *Lost Language of Symbolism Vol. II*, we find that Stonehenge *"...served thus as a gigantic timekeeper, chronometer, or clock."*[4] Stonehenge was a lithic representation of time[5] when studied three-dimensionally, counting angles, planes and corners. Stonehenge embodied the same geometrical relationships found at Newgrange.

Like the Great Pyramid, which was originally adorned in massive white limestone casing blocks, Newgrange in Ireland was originally covered in a layer of white quartz fragments so that it would be seen for miles in the sparkling Sunlight.6 As will be shown, the Great Pyramid was finished in 2815 BCE, or 1080 Annus Mundi, and interestingly, the tunnel length leading to the inner chamber wall is exactly 1080 Pyramid Inches.

These were calendrical monuments and this date is linked to the year the Watchers descended in 3439 BCE, being 276 years, or two Phoenix orbits of 138 years each. This period is 3312 months, or 552x6. As this is Enoch's 70th year prophesying against the Anunnaki, this is also the 210th year of the Olmec Calendar, or 70x3.

Knight and Lomas in *Uriel's Machine*, published textual evidence that the Book of Enoch relates that Enoch's location was at Stonehenge's latitude, as conveyed in the astronomical text.[7]

1. Sacred Number: Richard Heath p. 81; 2. Symbols, Sex and the Stars p. 256; 3. Beyond 2012 AD, citing Robert Heath; 4. Lost Language of Symbolism Vol. II p. 192; 5. Lost Language of Symbolism Vol. II p. 222; 6. Primitive Mythology p. 430; 7. Book of the Damned p. 146.

3162 BCE (733 AM): 5267 Before Armageddon/ 923 Before Flood/ 2077 Nemesis Cataclysm/ 1147 Phoenix Year

As mentioned in previous section (3163 BCE), astrophysicists Tom Ray of the Dublin Institute for Advanced Studies discovered that light would penetrate the back wall of the famous Newgrange vault exactly 5150 years before his calculation at the exact moment the Sun emerged.[1] This time indicates 3162 BCE (732 AM= **3163 BCE**) which virtually aligns with the other pre-cataclysm calendars that all began circa 3100 BCE.

Stonehenge's 29.5 monoliths in the outer sarsen circle mirror the 29.53 days between full moons.[2]

Charcoal samples taken from Newgrange's ancient caulking of the roof slabs date to about 3100 BCE.[3]

1. Feats and Wisdom of the Ancients p. 87; 2. Lost Cities of Atlantis, Ancient Europe and the Mediterranean p. 355; 3. Lost Cities of Atlantis, Ancient Europe and the Mediterranean p. 434.

3151 BCE (744 AM): 5256 Before Armageddon/ 912 Before Flood/ 2088 Nemesis Cataclysm/ 1158 Phoenix Year/ 888 Capture of Luna/ 288 Anunna Arrival/ 222 Olmec Calendar

In this year, King Enoch of the Sethites is elected by the people to be Emperor over 130 kings and princes, establishing peace between all kingdoms. This is the result of his fame and wisdom and belief that he is in direct communion with God.[1] His empire would last 243 years,[2] paralleling the 243 years from Enoch's first regnal year as a king in 3208 BCE to the death of Adam in 2965 BCE.

This unique year is found encoded within the chronometrical dimensions of the Great Pyramid, a fact borne out in *Chronotecture*. The calendrics for this year reveal some intriguing Golden Proportion sequences. 2088 of the Nemesis Cataclysm timeline is 1044+1044 years, 144 being a Golden Proportion number demonstrated easily by the Fibonacci spiral. This year is the 888th year of the Capture of Luna timeline, the 888th time the planet Earth had circled the Sun since it had adopted this new orbit is likewise a Golden Mean number, as is the 222nd year of the Olmec Calendar. This year is 288 years (144+144) after the Descent of the Watchers in 3439 BCE.

In this year, King Enoch of the Sethites is made emperor over 130 other kings and princes by voluntary consent. He establishes peace between warring kingdoms, his appointment due to his fame, wisdom, and communion with God. (Jasher 2:9-12) He would rule as Emperor for 243 years until his ascent to heaven, this 243 years paralleling the 243 years from Enoch's first regnal year as a Sethite king in 3208 BCE and Adam's death in 2965 BCE. (Jasher 2:17)

Enoch became Emperor in 744 AM, exactly 246 years before the Sethites (as per the prophet's instructions) began building the Great Pyramid in 990 AM.

"If it can be shown that the design of the Great Pyramid embodies a prophetic chronology, then we have the very evidence which God Himself declared would be proof that the design is from Him."[2]

1. *Jasher 2:9-12*; 2. *Jasher 2:17*; 2. *Biblical Antiquities III p. 56 – E. Raymond, Capt.*

3121 BCE (774 AM): 5226 Before Armageddon/ 882 Before Flood/ 2118 Nemesis Cataclysm/ 1188 Phoenix Year/ 918 Capture of Luna/ 318 Descent of Watchers/ 252 Olmec Calendar

Mayan Itza Temple of the Cross calendar began in this year with the ascension of a goddess who was 800 years old (myth). As will be shown, this is a memory of a Nephilim mother goddess matriarch, probably a female Anunnaki queen. Her dynasty would begin after Enoch was gone. She is remembered in the Americas as Spider Woman (8 legs), old Woman Weaver, and in India she was called Kali, who had eight arms. This is the 252nd year of the Olmec Calendar, 252 years being a sum that separates many major events in world history. Birthdate of Mayan Lady Beast.[1]

1. *Twilight of the Gods, p. 152.*

3113 – 3000 BCE

3113 BCE (782 AM): 5218 Before Armageddon/ 874 Before Flood/
   2126 Nemesis Cataclysm/ 1196 Phoenix Year/ 926 Capture
   of Luna/ 260 Olmec Calendar

This year is the start-date of the <u>Mayan Long-Count Calendar</u>, the most startling calendrical system from the ancient world, and most miscalculated and misunderstood. The Mayan Calendar is a timeline that counts down to the next year when Earth will be removed from its current place orbiting the Sun; when it will assume a <u>new</u> orbit around the Sun in 2046 CE. So much disinformation has been published about the Mayan system that even scholars have been led to believe that the calendar ended in 2012 CE, which is an impossibility. The Sethites under Enoch were extremely advanced chronologists who knew more about the Last Days than we do.

The future judgements and countdown until then were always measured in <u>days</u>, not years. As found numerous times in the cuneiform tablets of the Sumerians and other ancient Near East cultures, time was reckoned by the passage of days. Even the future Apocalypse was known as the Last <u>Days</u>, not Last Years. The first recorded element of time measurement in Genesis was *"the evening and the morning was the first <u>day</u>."* The correction of this error allows us to see that the Anunnaki descended not 432,000 years before the Flood, but 432,000 <u>days</u> (shars), being 1200 years between their descent in 3439 BCE and the Deluge in 2239 BCE. The archaic Dutch *Oera Linda* texts read that during the pre-Flood world *"...the years were not counted."*[1]

This is Enoch's 160th year alive and in this year, 79 mysterious bluestones (representing the Anunnaki) are added to Stonehenge I. This is referred to as <u>Stonehenge II</u> and the added 79 bluestones (43 of which survive today) were found within the lintels and weigh from between 2 and 5 tons each. These, along with the original 81 sarsens of Stonehenge I, add up to 160 megaliths, mirroring the prophet-chronologist's age. This is also Enoch's 120th year prophesying against the Anunnaki. The message of Stonehenge II is revealed in *Anunnaki Homeworld* that after a period of 2400 years (864,000 days) the year would be broken in 713 BCE and the perfect 360-day years would become 365.25-day years. The Mayan Long-Count is precisely 1,872,000 days in length, being 13 baktuns, each baktun being 144,000 days. On the 1,872,000[th] day, *"time will collapse,"* the date referred to as 13.0.0.0.0. Careless scholarship resulted with the false end-date of 2012 CE.

Accurately Interpreting the Long-Count
The 360-day period to the Maya was called the tun, being the basis for Mayan prophetic time-keeping.[2] Zecharia Sitchin noted that the three methods of calculating the Long-Count all relate to the arbitrary number of 360.[3] Despite this revelation, the Sumerian scholar calculated the Mayan calendar under the corrupted 365.25-day year. He is not alone. Because scholarship ignores solid archeological and textual evidence that Earth's orbit was dynamically altered in 713 BCE when all the calendars of the ancient world changed from China to the Americas, the calculation of the 1,872,000 days under the wrong solar year of 365.25 days corrupted the end-date to be in 2012 CE, abbreviating the perfect 5200 years of 360 days each to 5125 years. The chronologists and astronomers around the world in 713 BCE added five EVIL DAYS to the end of their calendars to compensate for the change. The entire system has been calculated under the 365.25-day year when the 365.25-day calculation is only good for years after the 713 BCE cataclysm that altered the solar year. Prior to 713 BCE, the 365.25-day year was UNKNOWN to the ancients. A tun is 360 days, a baktun is 400 tuns, or 144,000 days and 13 of these cycles being 1,872,000 days.

13 Mayan Baktuns
2713 BCE **(1182 AM) 1ˢᵗ baktun (144,000 days)**
2313 BCE **(1582 AM) 2ⁿᵈ baktun (288,000 days)**
1913 BCE **(1982 AM) 3ʳᵈ baktun (432,000 days)**
1513 BCE **(2382 AM) 4ᵗʰ baktun (576,000 days)**
1113 BCE **(2782 AM) 5ᵗʰ baktun (720,000 days)**
713 BCE **(3182 AM) 6ᵗʰ baktun (864,000 days)**

864 is the Foundation of Time number, as seen clearly in 3031 BCE. In 713 BCE the Dark Satellite passes too close to Earth (lost moon of Nemesis X Object) and a flux tube, or similar anomaly, incinerates

185,000 Assyrian soldiers on their way to Jerusalem. A cataclysm alters Earth's orbital distance from the Sun enough to add 5.25 days to the year. The baktuns were 400 years, but now they are 394.5 years due to the lengthening of the time it takes Earth to get around the Sun. See 713 BCE for details.

319 BCE **(3576 AM) 7th baktun (1,008,000 days)**
76 CE **(3970 AM) 8th baktun (1,152,000 days)**
470 CE **(4364 AM) 9th baktun (1,296,000 days)**
864 CE **(4758 AM) 10th baktun (1,440,000 days):**

The synchronization of 864 Common Era (Anno Domini) calendar is another piece of evidence that the calendars of the world, though often unrelated, were instituted by Intelligent Design.

1258 CE (5152 AM) 11th baktun (1,584,000 days):
This is Annus Mundi year 5152, which reflects the exterior angle of the Great Pyramid at 51°51'52" formerly found in the perfect white limestone casing blocks that numbered 144,000.

1652 CE (5546 AM) 12th baktun (1,728,000 days)
2046 CE (5940 AM) 13th baktun (1,872,000 days):

The Mayan Calendar will be COMPLETE with the completion of the 13th baktun. The ancient world was divided between 12 regions, but the Americas were then unknown, with the 13th region being the origin of the Maya. The Maya were 13 clans living under the 13 heavens who originally lived in North America before they migrated to Central America.[4] In 2046 CE the civilization of North America will be obliterated by a disaster. The United States, which began as 13 Colonies of Britain, are a people racially and spiritual descended from the 13 Tribes of Israel, and believers of a New Covenant. The 13th tribe was Ephraim, the tribe of adoption (adopting foreign people is what made the United States what it is).

Using scientific data obtained from a convention of archeologists, astrophysicists, botanists and historians who convened in 1997 CE, Frank Joseph demonstrates in his research that in the year 3113 BCE a single or series of comet/meteorite impacts devastated North America, causing global quakes, temperature and climate changes, drought, and blanketing of cosmic dust. His conclusion is that a <u>cataclysm</u> began the Mayan Long-Count.[5] This aligns perfectly with this thesis, which demonstrates that a cataclysm will also <u>end</u> the Long-Count. There is evidence that the origin of Venus or the sight of a long tail trailing off Venus was seen in 3113 BCE.

The Mayan historian Morley wrote that the Mayan civilization is *"Lost in the remote past, not even the shadowy half lights of tradition illuminating its beginnings. The very earliest inscriptions literally burst upon us fully formed, the flower of long-continued astronomical observations expressed in a graphic system exceeding intricacy."*[6] Spinden wrote, *"It would be accepted as self-evident that the Mayan Calendar could not have sprung suddenly into being, based as it is upon exact astronomical facts and intricate mathematical calculations. There was no earlier civilization in the American field sufficient to furnish even the fundamental concepts of the calendar."*[7] This was the early opinion of the baffled scholars, but now it has been discovered that the Maya merely <u>preserved</u> this ancient calendar from the Olmecs. The discovery of a jade figurine with a calendar inscribed upon its stomach indicates to scholars the date of 3113 BCE, showing that this unique calendrical system antedated the Mayan and EVERY OTHER archaic American system spanning back to at least 1200 BCE. Jeanne Reinhart in *Science Digest* (Sept., 1967) wrote that, *"It is a masterpiece of mathematical knowledge, and it was the Olmecs, not the Maya, who developed it."*[8] Again, they are only one more discovery away from finding that the Olmecs didn't develop it, either. This 3113 BCE date was the 260th year of the Olmec Calendar, or 52x5. The entire length of the Long-Count was 5200 years – years that were 360 days each, or 52x100.

In *Uriel's Machine*, Knight and Lomas show how Enoch is connected to Newgrange and Stonehenge and that a <u>comet</u> impacted the Mediterranean Sea area about 3150 BCE (37 years off) causing a magnetic field perturbation, a conclusion totally independent of some discovery concerning approximately 2150 BCE, made by Prof. Liritzis of Rhodes University.[9] 3113 BCE was a New World Calendar.[10]

The Maya believed in seven creator gods under the Primordial God, Hunab Ku.

Ivar Zapp and George Erikson in 1998 CE wrote that it is apparent that some major event of global import occurred at this date, that it must have involved a celestial observation *"...to have so influenced sky watchers around the world that it acted as a catharsis for a new age."*[11]

1. Secret Cities of Old South America p. 367; 2. The Mayan Prophecies for 2012 p. 192; 3. The Lost Realms: Skywatchers in the Jungle; 4. Children of the Sun p. 351; 5. Survivors of Atlantis p. 55-60; 6. Children of the Sun p. 19; 7. Children of the Sun p. 19; 8. Our Haunted Planet p. 132; 9. Book of the Damned p. 64, 249, 296; 10. (The Cosmic Code); 11. Atlantis in America, p. 263.

3103 BCE (792 AM): 5208 Before Armageddon/ 864 Before Flood/ 2136 Nemesis Cataclysm/ 1206 Phoenix Year/ 936 Capture of Luna/ 336 Anunna Arrival/ 270 Olmec Calendar/ 10 Mayan Calendar

This begins the Kali Yuga Calendar of ancient India, known as the Black Age that began with the emergence of an 8-armed goddess, a bloodthirsty queen. Her symbol was an upside down pentagram.[1] She was remembered as the deity Kali by the Hindus, having 8 arms, a deity of destruction.[2] She is Spider Woman in old America but the early Egyptians recalled her as a male deity, the Scorpion King (8-armed arachnid). KALI is the feminine form of the Sanskrit KALA, meaning Time.[3] The Persians relate that on this date there was a disaster that involved flooding.[4] In 290 BCE (293 BCE to be precise) the Egyptian priest-historian Manctho studied the Egyptian *Old Chronicle* that cites 113 regnal descents in a 36,525 "year" period back to Pharaoh Scorpion. But the text is a code, as evidenced by the number 36,525, being the same as the solar year at that time: 365.25 days. Interestingly, this sum is decoded by dividing it by 13 lunar months, the lunar year, which gives us 2810 years before 293 BCE, for the date of 3103 BCE.[5] In this year the chronologist king Enoch was 170 years old. This was the 130th year of his prophesying against the Anunnaki and his 48th year as Emperor. Kali is a fragment memory of the Anunnaki Dynasty that was then emerging but not yet in power – at least not over the Sethites. The date 3100 BCE is the time assigned by Egyptologists to the rule of Narmer, who unified all the people into a United Kingdom.[6] Narmer is in fact Enoch, described with the epithet NAR (NER is the same, representing 600: an epoch) and MER, the Egyptian designation for pyramid, with 3100 BCE being Enoch's 108th year of rule as a king.

Vedic *Puranic* texts read that the Kali Yuga Age would end after 3100 years with the appearance of a Savior King, the Great Saka, who will remove wickedness from Earth.[7] This 3100 year age counts down to 2

BCE birth of Jesus (**3103-3100 = 3BCE**). Tradition attests that it was this Great Saka that the Persian Magi sought when Jesus was born.

The calendrics of 3103 BCE further support its calendrical import. The Kali Yuga Age began in the year 792 Annus Mundi, 792 being the total orbit of the Nemesis X Object, the Kali Yuga being the beginning of Anunnaki rulership over part of humanity. This was 864 years before the Flood, the sum of 864, being a number that links both time and space like no other number as seen in 3031 BCE. Also, 3103 BCE is 5208 years before Armageddon, when the Anunnaki are defeated by the Chief Cornerstone in 2106 CE, with 5208 years being 744x7 or 434x12. As will be shown in this research, a period of Judged Time is 434 years, or 62 "weeks" of years in biblical eschatology. The Black Age begins a countdown to the end of Anunnaki dominion.

1. The Secret Doctrine p. 6; 2. The Illustrated Book of Signs and Symbols p. 20; 3. The Oxford Illustrated Companion p. 183; 4. Survivors of Atlantis p. 58; 5. Secret Cities of Old South America p. 408; 6. The Destruction of Atlantis p. 193; 7. Round Towers of Atlantis p. 345, citing Asiatic Researches.

3102 BCE (793 AM)

Scholars are at variance over the start of the Kali Yuga Age, some believing it began in 3102 instead of 3103 BCE. Because some consider this as Year One of the Kali Yuga, then the start-date of 3103 BCE is precise.[1]

1. Children of the Sun, p. 422.

3100 BCE (795 AM)

This is the scholarly-imposed approximate for the Narmer Palette, also known as the Victory Tablet of King Menes, which depicts a smooth-sided pyramid that Zecharia Sitchin holds as proof that even at this early date the concept of the pyramid was known.[1] The true date is 3103 BCE. It is to be noticed that between 3163 BCE and 3103 BCE, the world's most mysterious and well-preserved calendrical systems were all begun.

3163 BCE Newgrange & Stonehenge I (Enoch 110 years old).
3121 BCE Mayan Itza Temple of the Cross (Enoch 152 years old).
3113 BCE Mayan Long-Count (Enoch 160 years old).
3103 BCE Vedic Kali Yuga Calendar (Enoch 170 years old).

It is not without significance that the three timelines from 3121 BCE to 3103 BCE are all begun within 18 years of each other and are all systems employing ages measured in multiples of 144,000 <u>days</u>, 288,000 days, 432,000 days, etc.

Archeologists have marveled at the sudden transition from Neolithic culture to full-fledged civilization in Egypt at this [approximate] time.[2] This is the estimated time for civilization at Ban Chieng in northern Thailand that manufactured bronze tools and jewelry.[3] In south Thailand are unexcavated archaic megalithic ruins spread about, that local legends call the Empire of Langkasuka. Technolithic megaliths with precision articulation lie strewn about at Yarang, Pattani in southern Thailand.[4]

Puma Punku in South America is technolithic, estimated to have been built at this approximate date.

1. *Journey to the Mythical Past, p. 16-17; 2. Atlantis in America, p. 222; 3. Lost Cities of China, Central Asia... p. 15; 4. ibid. p. 19.*

3073 BCE (822 AM): 5178 Before Armageddon/ 834 Before Flood/ 2166 Nemesis Cataclysm/ 1236 Phoenix Year/ 966 Capture of Luna/ 366 Anunna Arrival/ 300 Olmec Calendar/ 40 Mayan Calendar/ 30 Vedic Calendar

The Nemesis X Object reached <u>aphelion</u> (furthest distance from the Sun) after travelling away from the inner solar system, far out in the Kuiper Belt, for 366 years since passing over the ecliptic in 3439 BCE. It now begins to journey back toward the inner solar system. This is the 200th year of the life of Enoch.

3067 BCE (828 AM): 5172 Before Armageddon/ 828 Before Flood/ 2172 Nemesis Cataclysm/ 1242 Phoenix Year/ 972 Capture of Luna/ 372 Anunna Arrival/ 306 Olmec Calendar/ 46 Mayan Calendar/ 36 Vedic Calendar

Planet Phoenix enters the inner solar system, completing its 138-year orbit and begins to journey back out into the Kuiper Belt. This was the second time that Phoenix entered the inner solar system since Enoch was alive. As Phoenix is the Planet of Chronology and Enoch was famous for being a seer-chronologist, the two facts do not seem to be unrelated. This year is the exact midpoint of Antediluvian History, being 828 years after man was banished from Eden in 3895 BCE and 828 years to the Great Flood in 2239 BCE. This is 46 years after the start of the Mayan Temple of the Cross Calendar. The calendrical overlap between BCE and original Annus Mundi dating is two and a half months because BCE is based off of a January 1st New Year's Day and the Annus Mundi New Year's is the vernal equinox at March 21st of the modern calendar. So at some point in this year is the 552nd year (**46x12**) of Mayan Chronology.

3039 BCE (856 AM): 5144 Before Armageddon/ 800 Before Flood/ 2200 Nemesis Cataclysm/ 1270 Phoenix Year/ 1000 Capture of Luna/ 722 Jewish Calendar/ 400 Anunna Arrival

Sitchin wrote that 288,000 "years" before the flood the Anunnaki manufactured mankind.[1] He was stuck on this 288,000 year theory, which is preposterous. 288,000 days is 800 years. This same 800 years is attested to in *Native American Lore*. Sitchin wrote that this was the Adamu who were created as laborers 80 sars before the Flood, which he again asserts was 288,000 "years."[2]

In the Assyrian record of the Seven Sages before the Flood (*Sages of Eridu*), Utu-Abzu was the seventh sage, and he *"who to heaven ascended."*[3] A German Professor, Rykle Borger, concluded in the *Journal of Near Eastern Studies* that he was the Assyrian "Enoch."

In the Sumerian List, Enmeduranki was Seventh.[4] Just like Enoch, he was taken into heaven and taught secrets.[5]

The Sumerian King List records that Enmeduranki reigned 21,600 "years" in Sippar.[6]

In foisting upon his readership such impossible "historical" records preserving timelines of 432,000 and 288,000 years, it is beyond explanation as to how so meticulous a scholar could make this error – especially when considering that in *Divine Encounters* on page 67, Sitchin wrote that, *"...it ought to be noted that 21,600* [Enmeduranki's reign] *reduced by a factor of 60 results in 360."* This duplicity is amazing in trying to fit Sumerian chronology into a uniformitarian mold. It seems Mr. Sitchin has cherry-picked his mathematical divisors to suit his theories.

Sumerian King List text W-B 62, kept at Ashmolean Museum, Oxford, states that Ziusudra [Flood Hero] reigned 36,000 "years" till the Flood.[7] The Sumerian King List records that the Kish Dynasty consisted of 23 kings who ruled for 24,510 "years," 3 months and 3½ days.[8] This is an arbitrary sum requiring a simple divisor of 360 to understand, providing us a dynastic duration of <u>408 years</u>.

Laboring Anunnaki revolt against their authority 400 years after their descent in 3439 BCE. Sitchin calculates this as 40 shars of 3600 "years" each. For a period of 144,000 years,[9] however, this 144,000 is actually <u>days</u> of a 360-day pre-Flood year (144,000÷260=400 years, the same as a Mayan Baktun). The rebellion was 800 years before the Flood.

1. *Divine Encounters p. 43;* 2. *Ibid p. 46;* 3. *Ibid p. 58;* 4. *Ibid p. 66;* 5. *Ibid p. 66;* 6. *Ibid p. 67;* 7. *Ibid p. 85;* 8. *Ibid p. 111;* 9. The 12th Planet p. 340.

<u>3031 BCE</u> (864 AM): 5136 Before Armageddon/ 792 Before Flood/ 2208 Nemesis Cataclysm/ 1278 Phoenix Year/ 1008 Capture of Luna/ 408 Anunna Arrival/ 72 Vedic Calendar

After 330 years below the ecliptic, the Ancient Earth-Killer Comet Group enters the inner solar system, passing close to Earth, illuminating the skies. This year is of great calendrical significance. It was Enoch's 120th year as Emperor and as it was 864 Annus Mundi, it began a 792-year countdown to the Great Flood in 2239 BCE, with 792 being the orbital period of the Nemesis X Object. This year was 2208 of the Nemesis Cataclysm, or 552x4 years, and 408 years since their descent to Earth, or 2448+2448 months. In Egypt, the number for "catastrophe" was 2448 as seen in 1447 BCE.

The number 864 links time and space and is the most important of all calendrical numbers. It is the mathematical nexus between all the world's calendrical systems based on the numbers 6, 12 and 144, a Golden Proportion number. In time and space, it relates to the <u>movement of the Earth</u>:

A day	(86,400 seconds)
60 days	(86,400 minutes)
360 days	(8,640 hours)
24 years	(8,640 days)
72 years	(864 months)

The sum of 864 is 432+432, or 144x6 or 108x8. As the Earth orbits the Sun every 864 years, the Zodiac retrogrades 12 degrees in the cycle of precession, a degree being 72 years. Eleven degrees is 792 years. This occurs as Earth travels along the ecliptic plane at 66,600 mph around the Sun.[1] The Sun's radius is 432,000 miles, giving it a diameter of 864,000 miles, about 108 times the diameter of Earth minus 8640 miles. Earth's own equatorial diameter before the Flood was 7920 miles, but the equatorial bulge was caused at the Great Flood in 2239 BCE, increasing this girth by 6.41 miles.[2] The Earth is 93,000,000 miles away from the Sun and by these unusual facts, seems to be commensurate. Because of the size of the Sun, the size of the Earth, and the distance between them, the dark shadow behind the Earth pointing away from the Sun, called the umbra, always points away from the Sun at a distance of 864,000 miles. The umbra is the region of total shadow, unlike the penumbra, which is partial shadow. This year of 3031 BCE is also the 864th month of the Vedic Calendar.

This date concerns something of importance to the Anunnaki, perhaps a sign or the start of a movement. Three calendars all relating to the Anunnaki involve this date – the Nemesis Cataclysm, the Anunna Arrival, and the Vedic Calendar. As this is years before the Flood, here too is an Anunnaki-related countdown to the end of their dominion and kingdoms, at the Diluvian disaster of 2239 BCE.

By studying the architecture of the Great Pyramid, researchers were able to determine how long the Royal Cubit was. They discovered that the unit of measurement to lay out the monument would measure the circumference of the Earth out in 86,400,000 cubits.[3] Further, in Hebrew, the gematrical value of the words "world" and "all nations", as well as the word "habitation" all equal 432.[4] Combining these ideas, we get 864 for "whole inhabited world."

In this year began the Anunnaki Human Cloning Project, producing Homo sapiens laborers 408 years after the Descent of the Anunnaki in 3439 BCE. Human clones of Negroid, Mongoloid, Amerindic, and dark Caucasoid were all manufactured utilizing filtered and corrupted Cro-Magnon (Archaic Caucasoid) and Anunna DNA. The different slave stock was exported out to Anunna camps and labor-intensive projects.

Later, the Mongoloid DNA would be infused with more Anunna DNA to create a race of intelligent servants to attend them – the high Oriental from which the Chinese, Japanese, Vietnamese and other Asians are descended from, and the *"black-headed people,"* or <u>Sumerians</u>.[5]
This was 792 years to the Great Flood in 2239 BCE, which is 792 years before the Exodus in 1447 BCE. Herodotus was told by Egyptian priests that their written history dated back 11,340 years before his era.[6] The Egyptians, as will be demonstrated elsewhere with proof, inflated their chronologies. The 11,340 years is actually 1134 years before their present era, not Herodotus's time. Egypt, after the 2239 BCE cataclysm, began in 1898 BCE-1897 BCE (1.5 years after the great Dispersion catastrophe known as the Babel Tower incident), a great dispersion of Aryan people in different directions, mostly away from the Near East. Counting 1134 years from 3031 BCE is the First Year of Egypt after the Cataclysm, or 1897 BCE.
The clever Egyptian deception is exposed by the next chronological fact given to Herodotus. The priests took him to a temple and showed him the statues of 341 high-priests who had in turn succeeded each other.[7] But these 341 statues did not represent men, but years, just as the great busts of Easter Island represented years (see 1687 BCE). This was 341 years, the precise duration from the Great Deluge Cataclysm of 2239 BCE to the founding of post-Diluvian Egypt in 1898 BCE. Remember, the Genesis account reads that the Flood lasted almost an entire year, thus, the 341 years ended in 1897 BCE. Ancient Sumerian and Babylonian temples had chambers with 360 statues representing the days of the year and Easter Island's engineers were attempting to commemorate the NER calendar of 600-year periods, famous in antiquity, when their project was violently ended in May, 1687 BCE by Phoenix cataclysm.

1. Fingerprints of the Gods p. 242; 2. The Energy Grid p. 86-87; 3. Atlantis in America p. 265; 4. Stones and the Scarlet Thread p. 51-52; 5. (The 12th Planet); 6. Atlantis: The Antediluvian World p. 108; 7. Atlantis: The Antediluvian World p. 108.

2999 – 2900 BCE

2965 BCE (930 AM): 5070 Before Armageddon/ 726 Before
>   Flood/ 2274 Nemesis Cataclysm/ 1344 Phoenix Year/
>   1074 Capture of Luna/ 148 Mayan Calendar/ 138 Vedic
>   Calendar

Adam died, the ancients tolling his years from Man's Banishment in
3895 BCE.[1] But Adam was created by the Anunnaki in 4039 BCE, 144
years priorly to 3895 BCE, thus the man actually outlived Methuselah
by 105 years, living 1074 years. On his deathbed, Adam gathered his
sons and a scribe was brought to record his prophecies. He related
that the Flood was coming and will kill everyone but eight people. He
ordered that his body was to be buried at the middle of the Earth (Giza:
see 2815 BCE), this being the Prime Meridian of the pre-Flood World.
He commanded that Seth was to carry out the project, his firstborn son
of the lineage that would be saved from destruction. Adam gave Seth an
ark with holy relics of gold, incense, and myrrh and declared that God
Himself had provided these artifacts as signs to mankind in the future.
These relics were to be preserved on the ark, a ship that would endure
the Deluge and afterward be placed in a city at the middle of the Earth.
Though he predicted that the city would be destroyed and plundered
after the Flood, the relics would be preserved *"...until the Word of God,
made man shall come,"* and kings shall offer the gold, incense, and
myrrh as tokens of his holy divinity.[2] Adam died in the 243rd year of
Enoch's reign, the prophet-emperor separating himself for long periods
of time to be instructed by God about the future of Earth.[3] Though
news of Adam's death was not known immediately, the inhabitants of
the Earth knew that something dreadful had happened because at the
same hour, the Sun darkened in daytime.[4] This is the FIRST time in
history of any record of the Sun darkening, which would not have been
the moon, but that of a celestial object transiting between the Sun and
Earth, darkening our world in shadow. Having spent 66 years above

the ecliptic, the Ancient Earth-Killer Comet Group now begins its 330-year orbit below the ecliptic, for a total orbital duration of 396 years, half of Nemesis X Object's orbit. The comet group fractured away from Nemesis X Object and the 66 years over the ecliptic is exactly 792 months.

The 930 years of Adam's life from his banishment until death parallels the length of Anunnaki history from 5239 BCE, the beginning of their chronology, to the destruction of the Daystar in 4309 BCE that ended the binary system. It destroyed whole planets and rearranged the entire solar system. Recall that 930 years is the product of both orbital periods of Nemesis X Object (792) and Phoenix (138). With Adam's death, God intends to fulfill His promise to His first earthborn son, that He would have an altar erected for Him as a sign to all generations that Adam, and by extension, humanity, was forgiven. As seen in 2815 BCE, this altar is the Great Pyramid.

Since the establishment of an Anunnaki matriarch in 3103 BCE, 138 years has now passed (a Phoenix orbit), or 1656 months (552x3). Also, the 148 years of the Mayan Calendar is 1776 months, with 1776 being a number encoded many times within the geometrical measurements of the Great Pyramid and found in timelines throughout history involving the Abrahamic, Israelite descendants of the Sethite lineage.

1. *Genesis 5:5*; 2.*Book of Adam and Eve II: 8:9-20*; 3.*Jasher 3:17*; 4.*Tales of the Prophets, p. 84.*

2944 BCE (951 AM):

The Chinese Shu-King text relates that Fu-Hi lived, an Oriental Noah.[1] (This text, also known as *The Book of Historical Documents*, and as *Shujing* in Chinese, dates back to the Zhou Dynasty, 1046-256 BCE.) This anachronism conveys that some ancient Chinese chronicler knew the duration of Noah's life to be 950 years, and this chronicler had access to an ancient calendar similar to the Annus Mundi, Year One. So Fu-Hi's life, or Noah's, according to this text, began in 3895 BCE and ended in 2944 BCE – a date that is 1 year off from 950 years after Man's Banishment. There is more evidence in this research exhibiting that the early Chinese once had access to accurate ancient chronologies.

1. *The Great Pyramid: Its Divine Message, p. 285.*

2929 BCE (966 AM): 5034 Before Armageddon/ 690 Before Flood/ 2310 Nemesis Cataclysm/ 1380 Phoenix Year/ 1110 Capture of Luna/ 510 Anunna Arrival/ 444 Olmec Calendar

Planet Phoenix passes through the inner solar system, completing its 138-year orbit on its way back out to the Kuiper Belt.

Phoenix transit is 24 years before the Great Pyramid construction began in 2905 BCE. In 138 years, Phoenix will transit again in 2791 BCE, precisely 24 years after the Giza complex in Egypt is completed in 2815 BCE.

2921 BCE (974 AM): 5026 Before Armageddon/ 682 Before Flood/ 2318 Nemesis Cataclysm/ 1388 Phoenix Year/ 1118 Capture of Luna

At age 352 Enoch fathers a daughter named Naamah.[1] She will later be married to the famous Noah, who is 82 years younger than her. Naamah's three world-famous sons would be named Japheth (Iapetos), Shem, and Ham (Chem) and be born before the Flood. Naamah is destined to acquire an infamous life after the Flood. She is recorded as one of the most wicked women of antiquity, as will be shown.

1. Jasher 5:15-16.

2909 BCE (986 AM): 5014 Before Armageddon/ 670 Before Flood/ 2330 Nemesis Cataclysm/ 1400 Phoenix Year/ 1130 Capture of Luna/ 204 Mayan Calendar

Strange dreams and omens afflict the kings and princes and priests, and Enoch assembles all of them,[1] a remarkable fact preserved also in the Coptic records and preserved by Arab scholars.[2] It is concluded in a council that a terrible disaster is going to come upon all mankind and Enoch secludes himself for many days until God reveals to him divine instructions of an architectural project. Enoch is to pass on the plans for his people to build immense constructions of stone at Achuzan (Giza) at the middle of the Earth. Enoch passes on these instructions. Enoch reveals that he is to depart – that he will be seen on Earth no more, and the masses grieve.

Calendrically, this is a revealing year. The Sumerian King Lists specifically record that this date, 670 years before the Flood, was the start-date of Alulim, the first of the Anunnaki Dynasty to rule over Earth. The title Alulim denotes a female demon (alu). This further explains the paradox of the Eight and Seven Kings of the Anunnaki. Popularly known throughout hundreds of ancient references, they are called the Seven Kings, powerful Anunnaki rulers over mankind, but the lists always have an Eighth title.

Alulim reigns for 28,800 shars (evenings and mornings: <u>days</u>), or 80 years. Her first 70 years of rule over the Canaanites and their kingdoms, as well as the Nephilim nations and giants, is insignificant until 2839 BCE. The latter 10 years of her reign even included ruling over the unwilling Sethite kingdoms, formerly under Enoch. She rules from the pre-Flood city Eridu, erected by Irad (a son of Cain). This year is 204 years of the Mayan Calendar, which counts down to a total Anunnaki Invasion in 2046 CE and global disaster (like their first appearance in 3439 BCE, killing a third of mankind). This 204 years is <u>2448 months</u>, again, the Egyptian number 2448 denoting <u>cataclysm</u>. It will be shown in this research that the sum of 670 years concerns EMPIRES and their beginnings and endings. This Anunnaki matriarch initiates her rule 670 years before the Deluge.

Charles Fort in 1919 CE wrote, *"...beings from other places have come to this earth...some of the more degraded ones have felt at home here, and have hung around, or have stayed here... concealing their origin, of course; having perhaps only a slightly foreign appearance."*[3]

Phoenix is <u>named</u> in a cryptic passage by Nostradamus concerning the end of a 670-year period. *"Many will die before <u>Phoenix</u> dies, until 670 his dwelling shall endure..."* This 670 years concerns the 670 years of Anunnaki supremacy on earth in the Sumerian King List. From 1909 BCE to the Flood Nostradamus specifically wrote in a letter that the Flood occurred after a <u>1242-year</u> period, revealing a knowledge about Phoenix's 138-year orbit.

Anunna kingship begins 670 years (241,200 days/shars) before the Flood of 2239 BCE, and the Anunnaki Dynasty beginning at Eridu, with two kings lasting 180 years, to 2729 BCE.

1. Jasher 3:10; 2. Origin and Significance of the Great Pyramid p. 104 Appendix; 3. The Complete Works..., Lo! p. 574.

2908 BCE (987 AM): 5013 Before Armageddon/ 669 Before Flood/ 2331 Nemesis Cataclysm/ 1401 Phoenix Year/ 1131 Capture of Luna

This is the 243rd year of Enoch's Empire, exactly 300 Years (108,000 days) since he had begun to rule over the Sethites. Enoch goes to a place called Achuzan (Giza), where he is taken up into the sky before 800,000 people. It is said that Enoch never died and that he would return to Earth in the Last Days to execute a prophetic ministry against the Watchers during the Apocalypse.[1] It is also declared that Enoch departed in the same hour and day that he was born, 365 years earlier.[2] The people assembled and the words and instructions of Enoch were read aloud. They were to follow the divine instructions in building a gigantic monumental complex at that same site. As the Anunnaki had determined to rule over Men on Earth, the Creator took Enoch into heaven to rule the faithful Anunnaki (angels) that had kept their divine estates.

Charles Fort in *New Lands* wrote, *"One supposes that if extra-mundane vessels have sometimes come close to this earth, then sailing away, terrestrial Aeronauts may have occasionally left this earth, or may have been seized and carried away from this earth."*[3]

1. *Genesis 5:23-24, Secrets of Enoch XLIV, Jasher 3:31-32; 2. Secrets of Enoch LXVII 5; 3. The Complete Works…, New Lands p. 521.*

2905 BCE (990 AM): 5010 Before Armageddon/ 666 Before Flood/ 2334 Nemesis Cataclysm/ 1404 Phoenix Year/ 1134 Capture of Luna/ 534 Anunna Arrival/ 208 Mayan Calendar

The Sethite architects surveyed the Giza plateau area and began quarrying stone from many miles away and the builders began the Altar of God. As the plateau was levelled, an elaborate and deep tunnel system with great galleries of rock and subterranean chambers was dug out. The four cornerstones were laid first. Then the outer perimeter of the Great Pyramid was laid. Then the erection of the monument was from the four corners up and inward. The beginning of construction from a distance appeared like four leaning towers of stone several courses high with the center of the pyramid, at all times of construction, the lowest. 51°51'52" angled sloping faces were carefully employed during the erection of more and more courses, added from the perimeters inward. As the structure was built up in elevation, the central portion remained like a cube, much lower than the four corners of the monument. The project will require 90 years (1080 months) to complete, in 2815 BCE, and its precision to the thousandths of an inch is far superior to structures erected by men in the 21st century. The distribution of the interior passages and chambers had long baffled researchers; however, the knowledgeable interpreter can read the measurements of the monuments as a great geometrical timeline of world history immortalized in stone. This is the subject of *Chronotecture*. This was originally theorized as early as 1859 CE and popularized from 1860 CE-1924 CE, but because these researchers were deficient in an accurate chronology of history, their exhibition of the theory fell short before the critics. The Pyramid Inch, based upon the velocity of the Earth around the Sun, is the basis for the length of measurement used in planning out the architecture of the Great Pyramid.

In this year, the Sphinx is carved out of the solid limestone of the Giza plateau. The statue is the largest to survive the ancient world and is a lithic prophecy of the diligent Watcher of Eden (Sphinx) which is a composite symbol for the Four Corners of Heaven – the Zodiacal Bull, Lion, Eagle and Man, that protects the Sacred Tree (Pillar of Knowledge) that mankind lost in 3895 BCE, but would regain in 2106 CE. Frederick Haberman, in *Tracing Our Ancestors*, wrote that *"The Sphinx is the most important symbol of Eden that we have left, or rather constitutes a link between Paradise Lost and Paradise Regained: for this Sphinx, with the body of a lion and the head of a woman, symbolizes nothing less that the Prophecy that from 'the seed of the woman shall come the Lion of the tribe of Judah to crush the Head of the Serpent, and for fifty-five* [actually 58] *centuries the Sphinx has been watching for Him."*[1] The early Egyptians of Thebes held traditions that the Sphinx had the body of a lion and a woman's head with eagles' wings.[2] Plutarch wrote that the Sphinx once had wings of a multi-colored hue.[3] There is a deeper connection between the Sphinx and the Genesis narrative. Planet Phoenix appeared as a fiery, flaming sword that in Genesis was the weapon of the Watcher, preventing mankind from regaining access to the Walled Enclosure, Eden. This guardian is immortalized as the Sphinx protecting the Great Pyramid site, ever-facing east. Remarkably, the Sphinx title derives from the same root from which Phoenix derives, so that *Sphinx* is actually the same word as S[Phinx], or s[Phoenix]. Remember the Gnostic text that declared that Phoenix was a witness against the angels.

The dimensions of the Sphinx at 240 ft. long with two outstretched limbs at a height of 66 ft. exhibits an architectural awareness of the entire length of the Nemesis Cataclysm of 7344 years, from 5239 BCE to 2106 CE when the Chief Cornerstone returns, the Stone the Builders rejected. The length of the statue at 2880 inches and its height of 792 inches (66 ft.), the orbital length of Nemesis X Object in years, we get 3672. This is precisely half of the 7344-year timeline. The measurement of 792 in the statue's height further links it to the Anunnaki. When considering the total intended height of the Great Pyramid with that of the Sphinx, a startling fact emerges. Once the top stone is laid upon the Great Pyramid, which today is flat, the monument with its casing stones would be 5814 inches high, and coupled with the 792 inch height of the Sphinx we get 6606 Pyramid Inches. 666 and its variants is a number expressive of the idea of total authority. 2905 BCE was exactly 666 years before the Flood in 2239 BCE.

In this year of 2905 BCE, the foundation of the pyramid was laid, this being 990 Annus Mundi. This year was 330x3. In Hebrew the gematria for "to make atonement" is 330, and anything multiplied by three in numerology represents totality, a fulfillment. Atonement requires an altar, and as will be seen in 2815 BCE, the Great Pyramid is the Altar of Adam, or more precisely, the Altar of Man. This year is 60 years after Adam died.

Egyptologists, using approximates, calculate their Egyptian Sothic Chronology as marking about 2895 BCE (10 years off) as a momentous event.[4]

"As respecting the pyramids and their purpose in the experience of the peoples... this occurs in the entrance of the Messiah in this period, 1998."[5]

1. *Tracing Our Ancestors* p. 63; 2. *The Greek Myths* p. 372; 3. *Return of the Serpents of Wisdom* p. 329; 4. *The Giza Prophecy* p. 144; 5. *Edgar Cayce's Story of the Origin and Destiny of man* p. 58, Edgar Cayce #5748-5.

2899 – 2800 BCE

2870 BCE (1025 AM):
The Egyptian Coptic records indicate that in the year 498 BCE golden tablets were interpreted that conveyed a history of the Great Pyramid with a description of its origin and purpose that counted back in time to the year 2870 BCE. The knowledge upon the golden tablets was supposed to have been copied from off the surfaces of the Great Pyramid. This Coptic chronology is fairly accurate, as this was the 35th year of pyramid construction at Giza. See 498 BCE.

2853 BCE (1042 AM): 4958 Before Armageddon/ 614 Before Flood/ 2386 Nemesis Cataclysm/ 1456 Phoenix Year/ 1186 Capture of Luna/ 520 Olmec Calendar/ 260 Mayan Calendar
Seth died in the 52nd year of construction on the Giza site at 912 years old.[1] As chief engineer and firstborn carrier of the Messianic bloodline, patriarch of the Sethites, he was buried somewhere at Giza. Two calendrical markers align perfectly with this 52nd year of pyramid construction. This was the year 520 of the Olmec Calendar, or 52x10, and the year 260 of the Mayan Calendar, or 52x5.

1. *Genesis 5:8.*

2852 BCE (1043 AM):
An ancient Chinese prophet in this year taught the people writing.[1] This is of particular interest because it was at this time that the lower multi-ton white limestone casing blocks were being prepared and dressed, with writings being placed upon them during pyramid construction. This knowledge was written by Enoch.
First Dynasty of China was of the Five Monarchs, in which there are actually nine rulers, a dynasty enduring 646 years to 2206 BCE.[2] NOTE: This is 24 years variance from the Sumerian King List, which shows the Anunnaki Dynasty of Seven Kings (other version is Ten Kings), which began 670 years before the Great Flood. This demonstrates that the Chinese tradition is the same as the Sumerian version.

Donnelly wrote, *"The early history of China indicates contact with a superior race. Fu-hi, regarded as a demi-god, founded the Chinese empire 2852 BCE. He introduced cattle... and taught the arts of writing."*[3]

1. The Antediluvian World p. 208; 2. Lost Cities of China, Central Asia and Arabia p. 384; 3. Atlantis: The Antediluvian World p. 208.

2844 BCE (1051 AM):
The golden tablets translated for King Phillipus in 498 BCE provided a second chronology concerning the construction of the Great Pyramid, dating the construction at 946 years prior to the arrival of the sons of Ham (Chem) into Egypt after the Deluge.[1] This migration took place in 1898 BCE (1997 AM), a year after the catastrophe remembered as the Babel Dispersion. This is the 61st year of construction at Giza.

1. Origin and Significance of the Great Pyramid, p. 112-114.

2843 BCE (1052 AM): 4948 Before Armageddon/ 604 Before Flood/ 2396 Nemesis Cataclysm/ 1466 Phoenix Year/ 1196 Capture of Luna/ 596 Anunna Arrival/ 270 Mayan Calendar/ 260 Vedic Calendar
Egyptian Coptic records date the construction of the Great Pyramid in this year, which was indeed the 62nd year of construction. The calendrics for this year are intriguing. It was 270 of the Mayan Calendar, or 3240 months (1080x3) and 260 of the Vedic Calendar, being 52x5, with the Vedic relating to the Anunnaki Dynasty. This Anunnaki Dynasty began in 2909 BCE, 66 years before this date, or <u>792 months</u>.

2839 BCE (1056 AM): 4944 Before Armageddon/ 600 Before Flood/ 2400 Nemesis Cataclysm/ 1470 Phoenix Year/ 1200 Capture of Luna/ 600 Anunna Arrival/ 534 Olmec Calendar/ 264 Vedic Calendar
This year marks the 66th year of pyramid construction, or <u>792 months</u>. Exactly 70 years earlier, the Anunnaki Dynasty began with a matriarch ruling over the Canaanite kingdoms in 2909 BCE but in this year, the empire of the Nephilim expands to include the Sethites. This is the 264th year of the Vedic Calendar, the Kali Yuga, which began with a wicked goddess. These 264 years, being 66x4, again provide us 792x4

months. The sum of 792 is the calendrical signature of the Anunnaki and Nephilim. Priorly in 3439 BCE, exactly 600 years earlier, the Anunnaki Watchers traded knowledge for the daughters of men, but they now take human females by force from their fathers and husbands. They also practiced hybridization between species of animals and plants.[1] The oldest stories of the Chinese concern the Dragon Kings who founded the first Chinese Dynasty. They descended from heaven and had flying machines. The founder of this dynasty was called Son of the Red Dragon.[2] The Dragon Kings were the firstborn sons of heaven and earth. In ancient Sumer the words heaven and earth were AN and KI, so these Dragon Kings were thus Anunnaki: [AN]unna[KI]. The same story is told in archaic records of India, and these machines that flew people around were named vimanas.

This begins the 600-year reign of terror of the Nephilim over mankind, which starts 600 years after their fathers appeared in 3439 BCE as the Anunnaki. The Nephilim were angel human hybrids, gigantic of stature and highly intelligent. This is 2400 years (600x4) after the Nemesis Cataclysm and 1200 (600x2) since Earth began orbiting this Sun. The famous hero Noah was born in the first year of the Oppression before the Flood, 2839 BCE, on the vernal equinox (anciently first day of the year).[3] He is named Menachem (Comforter)[4] and he is the fulfillment of a prophecy preserved by the Sethites concerning a man who would be born and save the world. As a type of savior, Noah was born in the year 1056 Annus Mundi, 1056 years after Man was banished from Eden in 3895 BCE. The sum of 1056 is the gematrical value of "the joy of thy salvation" in Hebrew, as found in Psalm 51:12.[5] In Greek, 1056 is the value for "the heavenly man," as found in 1 Corinthians 15:48. In a passage in Isaiah concerning the Great Pyramid (Isaiah 19:19-20), the statement in Hebrew, "He shall send them a savior and a great one," has the gematrical value of 1056. This Isaiah passage will be explained under the section 2815 BCE.

In 1895 CE the historian J.D. Parsons wrote that Noah's birth was *"... at the meeting point of two of those famous cycles of six hundred years so often referred to by ancient writers. "*[6] This refers to the Great Year, a 600-year period called by the Sumerians a NER. Long ago it was taught that a Divine Man would arise every 600 years.[7] Thus far this tradition has held true with the descent of the Watchers in 3439 BCE, a type of divine man, and the birth of Noah 600 years afterward. We will see that King David also fits within this timeline, as well as others. As Noah was born in the first year of the Oppression of the Sethites by the Nephilim, the pattern bears out later when Moses is born in the first year of the Oppression of the Israelites by the Egyptians. Incidentally, pre-Flood Sethite civilization was centered where Egypt was, geographically.

The Nephilim kings and overlords initiate new laws and policies. Ancient records attest that after Noah was born the world quickly fell into wickedness and experienced a great population explosion. Humanity turned wholly away from God and flourished in crime, incest, and corruption filling the earth with violence.[8] Hedonism became widespread among the Sethites now, and the practice of divorce became the norm, *"marrying wives and giving them up."*[9] Abortion became an accepted practice, *"...to kill an embryo in the womb"*, was taught by the Watchers.[10] Both divorce and abortion were Anunnaki population control methods employed against the Sethites, forcing humans to violate their principle command from God to *"be fruitful, multiply and replenish the earth."* Those holding to the Elder Faith became an extreme minority. The Nephilim matriarch would only rule over the United Empire of the Canaanites and Sethites for 10 years before her sons assumed the kingship in 2829 BCE, the famous Seven Kings of Sumer.

Charles Fort in *New Lands* wrote, *"Devils have visited this earth; foreign devils: human-like beings."*[11]

In the *Lamech Scroll* of the Dead Sea Scrolls, the birth of Noah troubled Lamech who claimed the child was not his. The baby looked different, but Lamech's wife swore she had not lain with one of *"the Sons of God."* Lamech's father Methuselah told him to accept this strange child as his own and called him Noah, destined to be the progenitor of a New Human Race.[12]

Enki's Homo Anunna interbreeding with Caucasian humans introduced Haplogroup X into the Homo sapiens genome, a distinct DNA marker... generally found only in Caucasians of northern European origin.[13]

Noah means rest. Noah reversed is AN(U). The *"rest"* refers to mankind's condition at this time. The slavery of the Anunnaki ended totally in 2647 BCE and humans had rest from their labors.

The Noah and Ark story may refer to the Flood of 3439 BCE when the An(Noah)nnaki arrived from the sea aboard an Ark (with seven men and a navigator), or descended by starship ark.

The Ark in the Sumerian version of the story is magurgur, or *"a very great ship."*[14]

In the Genesis Apocryphon, found in the *Dead Sea Scrolls*, the birth of Noah causes a controversy over his actual identity, his own father believing that Noah was not his son but that his wife had been visited by the Watchers (1Qap Gen. 2:1-7). Noah was chosen to father a newer humanity after the Flood because his physical body was the result of an additional genetic modification – he had more Anunnaki blood than other humans, as evidenced by his brighter eyes and skin in the Apocryphon.

Shemsu Hor were the Bronze Age Children of the Sun, a worldwide mariner dynasty with colonies spread abroad.

The Maya of Central America maintained a sophisticated, learned culture with historical records and traditions concerning a race of gods that manufactured humanity in a series of four stages in antiquity. The Church of Rome attempted to stamp out this knowledge but a text survived, The *Popul Vuh* of the Quiche Maya.[15] These four stages fit perfectly with the four Anunnaki NER epochs of 600 years each, between 5239 BCE to 4639 BCE, then to 4039 BCE, and 3439 BCE, to the final one in 2839 BCE when we have, in that EXACT year, the birth of Noah, the first appearance of white-skinned, blue-eyed humans among the indigenous dark-featured, smooth-skinned Adamu, exactly 600 years before the Great Deluge in 2239 BCE.

The Sumerian King List reads that kingship was first lowered from heaven to the city of Eridu. This place in Genesis is called Irad, from the root *descend*, found also in the name Jared, Enoch's father, a completely made up Jewish invention. The original text concerned the *descent of Enki* but the Jewish scribes in Babylon rendered it Enoch, descended from Jared.

The majority of extraterrestrial contactee accounts providing people today with *"alien"* versions of earth history describe the *"gods"* that came to earth as blond-haired, blue-eyed, Nordics – the gods of the

Sumerian tablets.[16] David Icke, citing the conclusions of a report by British Intelligence concerning 62,000 interviews with contactees, wrote that extraterrestrials benevolent to people claimed that *"...the original earth people were black, red and other native peoples in Africa, the Americas, Asia and Australia – not the white race."*[17] Icke concludes that the Nordic extraterrestrial humans then *"...interbred with their newly created races."*[18]

The white race is not the result of continued genetic experimentation but rather the product of centuries of Anunna visitors interbreeding with the Homo sapiens of their own manufacture... the planned campaign to generate on earth racial copies of themselves.

Much of the content of the Vedic literature, the earlier material, concerned conflicts between the agriculturalists, farmers and settlers, at odds with the nomad hunter-gatherers. Great wars are described between the Aryan settlers and others described as nomads.[19]

Max Muller wrote, *"The nations who are comprehended under the appellation of Indo-European – the Hindus, the Persians, the Celts, Germans, Romans, Greeks, Slavs – do not only share the same words and the same grammar, slightly modified in each country, but they seem to have likewise preserved a mass of popular traditions which had grown up before they left their common home."*[20]

Bonfey L. Geiger and other students of the ancient Indo-European languages believe that, *"the original home of the Indo-European races must be in Europe because their stock of words is rich in the names of plants, animals and names for seasons that are not found in the tropics or anywhere in Asia."*[21]

1. Jasher 4:18; 2. Odyssey of the Gods p. 30; 3. Jasher 4:13; 4. Jasher 4:13-14; 5. Stones and the Scarlet Thread; 6. Our Sun-God: Christianity Before Christ p. 33; 7. The Christ Conspiracy p. 338; 8. Jasher 4:16-17; 9. Luke 17:26-27; 10. Enoch 68:17-18; 11. The Complete Works of Charles Fort: New Lands, p. 301; 12. Twilight of the Gods p. 161; 13. The Ancient Giants Who Ruled America; 14. The Babylonian Theodicy p. 232; 15. Atlantis in America p. 168; 16. And the Truth Shall Set You Free p. 23; 17. ibid p. 23; 18. ibid p. 23; 19. Zoroastrianism p. 21-22; 20. Atlantis: The Antediluvian World p. 214; 21. Atlantis: The Antediluvian World p. 214.

2829 BCE (1066 AM): 4934 Before Armageddon/ 590 Before
    Flood/ 2410 Nemesis Cataclysm/ 1480 Phoenix Year/ 1210
    Capture of Luna/ 610 Anunna Arrival

The first son of the Anunnaki matriarch is Alalgar. His reign is recorded
in the Sumerian King List as 36,000 shars (evenings and mornings),
which is 100 years, with his reign ending in 2729 BCE. His reign
completes the 80 years (28,800 days) of the Erudu Dynasty begun by
his mother, the matriarch Alulim. She is considered the Genetrix of
the Seven Kings who were considered as gods to the Sumerians and
later Babylonians.[1] Though the Sumerians recorded 8 rulers they were
called the Seven Kings because the Genetrix was excluded.[2] This was
the 76th year of pyramid construction.

1. *Gerald Massey Lectures, p. 109;* 2. *Gerald Massey Lectures, p. 109-110.*

2815 BCE (1080 AM): 4920 Before Armageddon/ 576 Before
    Flood/ 2424 Nemesis Cataclysm/ 1494 Phoenix Year/
    1224 Capture of Luna/ 624 Anunna Arrival/ 558 Olmec
    Calendar/ 288 Vedic Calendar/ 24 Anunnaki Dynasty

The Great Pyramid of Giza and the complex is complete, requiring
90 years (1080 months) to complete from its start in 2905 BCE, this
1080 months mirroring this 1080 Annus Mundi year. This 90 years is
32,400 days, or 10,800x3 days. This 32,400 days is reflected in the
length of the original perimeter of the Great Pyramid's base, 3024 feet,
or 1008x3. Even today, as measured by Graham Hancock, it is 3023.16
feet.[1] The geometry of the pyramid further identifies its own date of
construction. The pyramid sits on a foundation of four corners, but the
monument was designed to have a fifth corner, the top stone, or apex.
The cornerstone. Geometrically, the five terminations of the pyramid
shape, when depicted one-dimensionally, exhibit a perfect pentagram
and the pentagram is composed of ten 108° angles. Thus, the five-pointed
pentagram is the geometrical sum of the number 1080. The year 1080
of the pre-Flood calendar was 2815 BCE. A close approximate for this
year was made in 1954 CE when George G. M. James wrote that the
Great Pyramid and Giza complex was constructed about 2800 BCE.[2]
A scientific bulls-eye. The Great Pyramid's dimensions record much
astronomical knowledge. One of these is found in that the combined
diameters of the Earth and moon, being 7920 and 2160 miles, is 10,080
miles. Bonnie Gaunt notes in her fascinating research that the precise

geometrical proportions of the Great Pyramid can be constructed on the diameters of the Earth and moon.[3] Also, because of the Earth-moon relations, such as distance and velocity around the Sun and the moon's movement around Earth, we find that the lunar umbra, the darkest part of the moon's shadow, bringing total darkness during an eclipse, travels across the face of the earth at a mean average of 1080 mph.

The 1080 pentagram geometry of the Great Pyramid has a mysterious link to the Sumerian symbol for something that falls out of the sky *"to break up the earth"* called the Plough Sign. Referred to in Sumerian as the AR UB, the pentagram symbol identifies a celestial body that drops from the sky to destroy the earth because God's harvest (humanity) has ceased bearing fruit. It must be recalled here that in 1924 CE, Davidson published his research on the geometrical distribution of the Great Pyramid's four cornerstones that unveiled a precise astronomical knowledge of a global timeline, the Capture of Luna, from 4039 BCE to 2046 CE when Earth will be pushed off its orbital belt by a large celestial body. Further, as will be seen in 2046 CE, a large object from space will slam into North America.

The sum 1080 is the gematrical value of the Hebrew statement in Isaiah 66:1 – "Heaven is my throne and earth is my footstool." Also, 1080 is the value of "The Lord is in His holy temple, let all the earth keep silence before Him."[4] We also read in Isaiah, *"God himself that formed the earth and made it."* This equals 1080. In the Greek gematria, the term Holy Spirit has the value of 1080. If the total circumference of a circle was 1080, then its diameter would be 344. Bonnie Gaunt notes that 344 is the gematrical value for "great wonder" in Greek, as well as "the Light of the World," as found in Matthew 5:14.

The four large cornerstones of the monument were highly polished white limestone megaliths, numbered among the 144,000 casing blocks of the monument. These blocks were 100 inches thick and with a tolerance so smooth, that modern architecture has not replicated. For a long time, scholars debated on the existence of these perfect blocks until, in 1837 CE, some of these surviving blocks buried at the base of the Great Pyramid were discovered by Col. Vyse's expedition. The blocks along the lower courses originally had whitened writings on them still easily seen and translated in the days of Abraham (see 1837 BCE-1825 BCE) and still noticeable in the days of the Greek historian Herodotus in 450 BCE. These blocks covered the interior limestone blocks that make up the Great Pyramid that we see today. The monument is exactly 203 levels of blocks, 203 being the gematrical value for "He created."[5] But 203 levels was not the intended height. With the placement of the Chief Cornerstone, the monument will be finished at 204 levels. The Chief Cornerstone represents a Divine Being that will sit atop the Monument of Man, the Stone the Builders (Anunnaki) rejected.

The priest-prophet Ezra wrote that the knowledge of God was preserved in the 204 Books, which is an analogy of the 204 courses of the Great Pyramid, when the Chief Cornerstone is placed atop it. The Phoenix Year from Man's Banishment in 3895 BCE counts 14 Cursed Earth periods of 414 years each (5796 years) to 1902 CE when planet Phoenix passed through the inner system, depositing millions of tons of cosmic dust and mud on Earth. 1902 CE is the last pass of Phoenix before it returns in 2040 CE and results in a pole shift, meteoric fallout, global flooding and earthquakes, and the death of 25% of humanity, known in the Revelation at the Sixth Seal. The actual levels of blocks of the structure form a chronometrical countdown that begins in the Last Days, starting at 1902 CE, a date also figuring prominently in the internal chronometry of the Great Pyramid, as found in the extensive charts of *Chronotecture*. Thus, 1902 CE begins a 204-year countdown to the RETURN OF THE CHIEF CORNERSTONE in the year 2106 CE, the same year that we have already seen is the 6000th year of mankind's banishment from Eden at 3895 BCE.

The length of 204 years is 2448 months, the Egyptian number designating cataclysm. It was in 2448 Annus Mundi (1447 BCE) that the Israelites escaped out of Egypt after the country was plagued with terrible disasters. This was the Exodus, also revealing that the 2448th month after 1902 CE (which will occur in 2106 CE) signifies a PLANETARY EXODUS.

The Chief Cornerstone will sit upon the flat area atop the monument that measures 48 ft. wide and 30 foot high. When capped with a cornerstone, the structure will measure 485 feet high. Bonnie Gaunt notes that the gematrical value for the statement, "There is no Rock like our God," found in 2 Samuel 2:2, is 485. Also, in Psalm 73:17, the words "the sanctuary of God," is 485, as well as the prophecy in Isaiah 60:19, which states, "The Lord shall be unto you an everlasting light." For the edification of the reader, a gematrical value is determined by a cryptograph that appears in the form of a word, with the hidden meaning of this word being determined by the value of the letters. This was often done intentionally for only those people who were able to decipher it.

The total geometrical height of the Great Pyramid (if the capstone is in place) is exactly 5814 Pyramid Inches, which is paralleled by an unusual astronomical fact. The peculiar shaft up and out of the structure has long been known to point at the Orion constellation, with Orion being an ancient Messianic symbol. John Gordon, in *Egypt: Child of Atlantis,* wrote, *"The maximum altitude above the horizon (during the cycle of precession) of the constellation <u>Orion</u> is 58°14' when it rises almost due east at azimuth 91°."*[6] Another *"coincidence"* is found in the research of Graham Hancock. In antiquity the Great Pyramid was the symbol in Egypt for the Gate of Rostau, a spiritual realm of the dead. The Egyptian epoch for when the spirits ruled long ago was 5813 years according to Manetho of Alexandria.[7]

Because the monument was never finished (the cornerstone was rejected) it presently stands at 5448 Pyramid Inches, which, amazingly, identifies a particular passage in the Bible that researchers have long suspected refers to the Great Pyramid, for other reasons. The following passage in the prophetic book of Isaiah has the gematrical value <u>5448</u>.

> *"In that day shall there be an <u>altar</u> of the Lord in the midst of the land of <u>Egypt</u>; and a <u>pillar</u> at the <u>border</u> thereof to the Lord. At it shall be for a <u>sign</u> and for a <u>witness</u> unto the Lord of Hosts in the Land of Egypt."*[8]

This refers to the Altar of Adam, placed at the center of the Earth, the zero-degree longitude and latitude, the prime meridian of the pre-Flood civilization known as the Pillar of Heaven, the central axis. Prior to Mohammedan times in Arabia, the pyramids were called <u>pillars</u>. In *Lost Scriptures of Giza* are chapters full of historical and archeological evidences and proofs that this passage refers to the Great Pyramid. Giza means <u>border,</u> and pyramids were <u>signs</u> and <u>wonders</u> in the land of Egypt according to Jeremiah the prophet. The Book of Enoch records that the chronologist-prophet wrote 366 *"books,"*[9] these *"books"* being no different than the 204 books of the prophet-priest Ezra. They are symbols of pyramid architectural dimensions. The Pyramid's present height at 5448 Pyramid Inches is exactly 366 inches under its intended height of 5814 Pyramid Inches when the Chief Cornerstone is placed. The pyramid as the central axis of the world at the middle of the Earth identifies it with Mount Meru in the eastern traditions, but also Mount MASU of Sumer, the Tree of Knowledge, the tree Yggsdrasil of the Scandinavians, Irminsul of the ancient Germans, etc. The present 5448 height as a calendrical code identifies the year 5448 Annus Mundi, or 1554 CE, the exact year that the prophecies of Nostradamus had Europe on fire with its startling and dire predictions. In *Nostradamus and the Planets of Apocalypse,* we find proof that this French prophet of Jewish ancestry was knowledgeable of planet Phoenix, its appearance in 1902 CE, and its return for a cataclysm in 2040 CE, as well as the second global disaster that will occur in 2046 CE, both dates encoded within the chronometry of the Great Pyramid.

As the Altar of Man (Adam) at the center of the earth, the Great Pyramid is referred to in Vedic writings of ancient India as the Altar of Agni. Like the Great Pyramid, it was covered with the Vedic scriptures, with knowledge on its stones, and these stones numbered specifically 10,800 bricks. This aligns with the Arabic traditions where we find that there is a Preserved Tablet from antiquity, a stone writing dating back to the Beginning of Time that contains all the prophecies, writings and knowledge. The angel of Death with 1080 eyes (360 eyes within three larger eyes) searches continually through the records, making sure no one dies before their time.[10]

Some time in Enoch's prophetic career, he had a vision of the Great Pyramid and its relation to the Tree of Life. He called it a mountain of Fire at the MIDDLE OF THE EARTH (the word pyramid means "Fire in the Middle"). He describes its stones as brilliant and beautiful, splendid to behold, and beautiful was its surface, which we know describes the original white polished casing blocks of the monument. An angel tells Enoch *"That mountain thou beholdest, the extent of whose head resembled the Seat of the Lord [Throne], will be the seat on which will sit the holy and great Lord of Glory [Chief Cornerstone], the everlasting King, when He shall come and descend to visit the Earth with goodness. "*[11] That Enoch fully understood the mystery of the Son of Man, the Christ, is clearly seen in Enoch 46:1-3, where we find him at the Court of Heaven beholding the Ancient of Days (Creator) and another figure named the Son of Man, who would come to Earth and break the power of the mighty and lay low the kings of the Earth. It was revealed to Enoch that the Son of Man was ancient, His name invoked in heaven before the Sun and stars were created. He (Christ) would be a support (pillar) for the righteous and shall *"...be the light of the nations.*"[12] The title for the Creator as Ancient of <u>Days</u> further supports the fact that the antediluvian civilization reckoned time by the passing of <u>days</u> as being the most important, then moons (months), and years.

That Enoch wrote that the Savior would be the Light of Nations links the Pyramid with the Egyptian name for the monument. The Great Pyramid was called Har-Khuti, or <u>Lord of Lights,</u> or lord of the Glorified Elect. The sign for Har-Khuti was the heptagram, the seven-pointed star. Intriguingly, the seven-point geometry is the only way to obtain the elusive 52-degree angle, and the structure at Giza was slanted at precisely 51°51'52", or 52°. Even the interior passage angles inside the structure are sloped at 52 degrees. The heptagram is mysterious because unlike other geometrical forms like squares and triangles, no two geometrical forms can combine to make it. Further, Har-Khuti was related to the Egyptian concept of <u>Eternal Word</u>.[13] Of course, this is another connection to the Chief Cornerstone, the Word made flesh.

The calendrics for this year of 2815 BCE (1080 already examined) demonstrates further unique characteristics for this time. The Great Pyramid was finished 576 years before the Deluge, or 144x4, with the sum of 144 being a Golden proportion number. This year was also the 288th year of the Vedic Calendar, being 144+144 from 3103 BCE, which marked the start of the Black Age with emergence of an Anunnaki matriarch's rule. This corresponds calendrically with the fact that 2815 BCE was the 24th year of the Anunnaki Dynasty over the Sethites, called the Oppression. This 24 years was <u>288 months</u>, paralleling the 288 years since 3103 BCE.

Hebrew for <u>piled up</u> is 366 (see Exodus 15:8). The Pyramid without its apex stone is 5448 inches high, or <u>366 inches</u> under Pyramid's geometrical height of 5814 inches.

Agni in the *Rig Veda* is said to have <u>Fire in his stomach</u>,[14] and the word pyramid literally means <u>fire in the middle</u>. Agni transports the dead to another realm and is associated with <u>immortality</u>. Agni is hidden within the <u>water</u>[15] – see 1899 BCE, Great Pyramid under the sea.

Blocks of the Great Pyramid are not chipped nor rounded at the corners, which would have occurred from being manhandled by brute force. M. Don Schorn notes that, *"...they appear to have been gently placed in position from above, as if weightless..."*[16]

The area of an atom is less than .0001% mass, the orbiting electrons moving at speeds so fast as to create a <u>shell</u> holding in <u>nothing</u>. Even the nucleus of the atom when magnified dissolves into an oscillating field.

So with mass, we have billions of spaces of .0001% mass that <u>do not</u> <u>touch</u> each other, which we refer to as <u>physical reality</u> – a vast backfield of empty space by which all perceiving phenomena manifests. This is <u>not</u> the <u>real</u> universe, but a containment shell, a <u>manufactured</u> illusion of reality referred to herein as the <u>holosphere</u>.

Thoth was called the Lord of <u>Eight</u>. Sitchin notes that these eights referred to eight celestial directions, including the four cardinal directions.[17] This refers to the <u>Great Pyramid,</u> which is actually 8-sided (there is a subtle, concaved indentation in the middle of each of the four sides, seen better from the air and first noticed in modern times by a British Air Force pilot in 1940). Campbell's shaft shows multiple levels of tunnel systems with squared corridors, through the solid bedrock of the Giza Plateau.[18]

Petrie submitted evidence of highly sophisticated machined lathing of Giza architecture, even cutting concave and convex spherical radii without splintering the material.[19] Petrie's findings were largely ignored and <u>unrecognized</u> because at the turn of the 19th-20th century, the technology required to produce the anomalies noticed by Petrie was unknown until it was bought to the public's attention by Christopher Dunn.

Petrie's measurements were conducted in 1880 to 1882.[20]

Arabic traditions hold that the Angel of Death has 360 eyes, each containing three more eyes,[21] or, a total of 1080 eyes. As many know, the word "angel" means *"messenger,"* and this 1080-eyed messenger of death gazes at the Preserved Tablet, a stone writing from the Beginning, containing the knowledge of both past and future. This 1080-eyed messenger of death makes sure no one is taken from the earth unless ordained by destiny.[22]

In ancient Greek traditions the Sphinx was born of Echidna and Typhon[23] Ty[phoen], or Phoen[ix]. Echidna was a celestial monster that resided in a cave (hidden in the sky) and was the consort of Typhon, which was the cause for much destruction. Thus, the Sphinx had its origin in the minds of early Greeks with the concept of cataclysm.

Will Hart (among others) wrote that there were 144,000 white limestone casing blocks on the Great Pyramid, similar to marble in hardness, with an average weight of 20 tons each.[24]

The Adites, according to Arabian traditions of the pre-Flood people, ordered the construction of a terrestrial paradise in the desert of Adan, called *"Irem of the Columns,"* the like of which has not been erected in these lands.[25] This Irem of the Columns is found in the Quran. The Adites were architects and builders who moved enormous blocks of stone.

Plato's ideal number of households in his city was 5040 [half of 10,080].[26] Remember, the scriptures read that "in my Father's house are many mansions..." and that Abraham looked for a city whose builder and maker was God... and that Abraham journeyed into Egypt. Ignatius Donnelly correctly relates that the Garden of Eden imagery, the pyramid, and Atlantis narrative are all connected in this vein.[27]

In 1950 CE Ignatius Donnelly wrote, *"The writer has seen numerous reports that the outer casings of the two large pyramids of Giza were originally covered with writings."*[28]

In 1301 CE, a powerful earthquake shook loose some of the white Tura limestone casing blocks of the Great Pyramid.[29] By 1360 CE the local Muslims and stripped off the rest for rebuilding materials.

At Angkor Wat in Cambodia, the Hindu tradition of good and evil at war is found carved in stone, particularly at the South Gate of Angkor Thom. This shows the cause of good and evil, with 54 gods pulling the serpent Vousaki in one direction, as 54 demons pull in the opposite direction as the serpent, or Naga, is wrapped around the Holy Mountain (Mount Meru). This conflict produced immortality.[30]

The Hopi believe their ancestors migrated through three worlds by the aid of Spider Grandmother.[31]

Stonehenge tradition holds that the megaliths used to build it were flown into place from a great distance.[32]

John Ivimy of Britain in his *The Sphinx and the Megaliths* notes that the Stonehenge architecture employed a numbering system based on the number 6, rather than the number 10.[33]

Ancient Egyptians used a 6-base numbering system.[34]

1. Fingerprints of the Gods p. 192; 2. Stolen Legacy p. 51; 3. Stonehenge and the Great Pyramid p. 81; 4. Isaiah 45:18; 5. Today, Tomorrow and the Great Beyond p. 456-457; 6. Egypt: Child of Atlantis p. 193; 7. Fingerprints of the Gods p. 405; 8. Isaiah 19:19-20; 9. The Book of Adam and Eve II 23:3; 10. Tales of the Prophets 14-15; 11. Enoch 24:1-2, 8, 25:1; 12. Enoch 48:2-3; 13. Gerald Massey Lectures p. 235; 14. An Introduction to Hinduism p. 46; 15. Ibid p. 46; 16. Elder Gods of Antiquity p. 31; 17. When Time Began p. 207; 18. Technology of the Gods p. 260; 19. Ibid p. 267; 20. Ibid p. 279; 21. Tales of the Prophets 14; 22. Tales of the Prophets 14-15; 23. Secret Cities of Old South America p. 292; 24. The Genesis Race p. 79; 25. Atlantis: The Antediluvian World p. 174; 26. Atlantis in America p. 218; 27. Atlantis: The Antediluvian World p. 273; 28. Atlantis: The Antediluvian World p. 279; 29. The Message of the Sphinx p. 37; 30. Mushrooms and Mankind p. 64-65; 31. In the Hands of the Great Spirit p. 12; 32. Lost Cities and Ancient Mysteries of Africa and Arabia p. 27; 33. Lost Cities of North and Central America p. 486; 34. Lost Cities of North and Central America p. 486.

2800 BCE (1095 AM): 4905 Before Armageddon/ 561 Before Flood

[approx.] Dr. R.M. de Jonge wrote, *"The circumference of the earth was very accurately known by circa 2800 BCE."*[1] Richard L. Thompson, Ph.D. in mathematics, found that numerous texts from ancient India gave accurate dimensions for the diameter of the earth and even the plane of the ecliptic.[2]

1. *How the Sun-God Reached America p. 4-12*; 2. *The Ancient Alien Question p. 115.*

2799 – 2700 BCE

2791 BCE (1104 AM): 4896 Before Armageddon/ 552 Before Flood/ 2448 Nemesis Cataclysm/ 1518 Phoenix Year/ 1248 Capture of Luna/ 648 Anunna Arrival/ 312 Vedic Calendar/ 48 Anunnaki Dynasty/ 24 Anno Pyramid

Planet Phoenix passed through the inner system, completing its 138-year orbit on its way back out to the Kuiper Belt. Though we have no records of Phoenix being sighted, the calendrics indicate that Phoenix was indeed seen and perhaps there may have been a transit, darkening the Sun. This year completes the 2nd 552 year Phoenix Cycle since Man's Banishment in 3895 BCE, being precisely 552 years before the Deluge. Interestingly, this year was 66.6% of the way through the Phoenix Cataclysm starting with Man's Banishment, to the Flood in 2239 BCE, and likewise, 66.6% of the Nemesis Cataclysm remains until they are destroyed in 2106 CE, the 6000th year of Man's Banishment. This year is the 2448th year of the Nemesis Cataclysm timeline, 2448 being the number for <u>disaster</u> (see 1447 BCE), and 2791 BCE is also 4896 years Before Armageddon, or 2448+2448 years. This Phoenix passing was exactly 360 years after Enoch had been made Emperor in 3151 BCE. Noah was 48 years old.

It is 138 years since Phoenix passed through the inner solar system in 2929 BCE, exactly 24 years before the Pyramid construction began in 2905 BCE. Phoenix now returns here 24 years <u>after</u> the Pyramids are completed in 2815 BCE.

2778 BCE (1117 AM):

This is the start-date for the Egyptian Short-Chronology,[1] remarkably only 37 years from the completion of the Great Pyramid.

1. *Civilization or Barbarism?, p. 281.*

2755 BCE (1140 AM): 4860 Before Armageddon/ 516 Before Flood/ 2484 Nemesis Cataclysm/ 1554 Phoenix Year/ 1284 Capture of Luna/ 684 Anunna Arrival/ 84 Anunnaki Dynasty/ 60 Anno Pyramid

Enosh died, the son of Seth, at age 905. Once a mighty king. When he ruled over the Sethites in 3439 BCE, the Anunnaki descended to Earth. Incidentally, this year of his death was 2484 of the Nemesis Cataclysm timeline, or 6 Cursed Earth periods of 414 years each, equaling 18 orbits of Phoenix.

2750 BCE (1145 AM):

Approximate date for completion of the Great Pyramid according to modern Egyptologists.[1] This date, however, is 65 years off.

1. *The Secret in the Bible p. 170.*

2729 BCE (1166 AM): 4834 Before Armageddon/ 490 Before Flood/ 2510 Nemesis Cataclysm/ 1580 Phoenix Year/ 1310 Capture of Luna/ 384 Mayan Calendar/ 110 Anunnaki Dynasty/ 86 Anno Pyramid

The second king of the Anunnaki-Nephilim Dynasty takes the throne, named Enmenluanna, his seat situated at the city of metalworkers called Badtibira. His Sumerian title, EN.MEN.LU.AN.NA signifies that he was a priest and Son of Heaven. His own reign would last 43,200 shars (evenings and mornings), or 120 years (**120x360=43,200**). Noah was 110 years old, his future wife, Naamah, being 192 years old. This year is 70x7 to the Great Flood.

The Anunnaki abandoned Eridu, moving kingship to Badtibira. This dynasty of three kings would last 300 years (108,000 days/shars), to 2429 BCE.

2713 BCE (1182 AM): **4818 Before Armageddon/ 474 Before Flood/ 2526 Nemesis Cataclysm/ 1596 Phoenix Year/ 1326 Capture of Luna/ 660 Olmec Calendar/ 400 Mayan Calendar/ 102 Anno Pyramid**

The first Baktun of 144,000 days of the Mayan Long-Count Calendar is complete from 3113 BCE, factored on the ancient year known to the Maya, the 360-day year. The Mayan system is also based on multiples of 52, and interestingly, this year is <u>520 years</u> from 3233 BCE. Enoch began prophesying against the Anunnaki. This is also the 408th year of the Maya Temple of the Cross Calendar that started in 3121 BCE, with 408 years being 2448+2448 months. Noah is 126 years old, Naamah is 208 years old (52x4).

2707 BCE (1188 AM): **4812 Before Armageddon/ 468 Before Flood/ 2532 Nemesis Cataclysm/ 1602 Phoenix Year/ 1332 Capture of Luna/ 732 Anunna Arrival/ 666 Olmec Calendar/ 396 Vedic Calendar/ 132 Anunnaki Dynasty/ 108 Anno Pyramid**

The Nemesis X Object ascends out of the Deep (south of solar system) after 732 years below the ecliptic. It passes through the inner system in the 22nd year of king Enmenluanna of Sumer. The calendrics for this year are astonishing. This is 108 years after the Great Pyramid was completed, and 1188 Annus Mundi, or 108x11, from Man's Banishment in 3895 BCE. It is 468 years before the Deluge, or 5616 months, which is 108x52 months. As this is the 1332nd year that Earth had orbited the Sun in its new astronomical position, this timeline is 666+666 years in orbit, and this year is also the 666th year of the Olmec Calendar. The Vedic Calendar has it at the 396th year, half of Nemesis X Object's orbit of 792 years. The Anunnaki Dynasty, which ruled over the Sethites beginning the Oppression, was 132 years earlier, or 792+792 months, in 2839 BCE at the birth of Noah. This year of 2707 BCE was precisely a Cursed Earth period of 414 years after the start of the Mayan Temple of the Cross Calendar in 3121 BCE. Nemesis X Object begins its 60-year journey north of the ecliptic.

2699 – 2600 BCE

2699 BCE (1196 AM): 4804 Before Armageddon/ 460 Before
Flood/ 2540 Nemesis Cataclysm/ 1610 Phoenix Year/
1340 Capture of Luna/ 740 Anunna Arrival/ 414 Mayan
Calendar/ 140 Anunnaki Dynasty/ 116 Anno Pyramid

This is the traditional beginning of Chinese civilization. The ancient
Chinese Calendar begins. It must be noted that the Chinese recall that
their own first dynasty began with the Dragon Kings (Anunnaki).
This year is almost identical to 600x8 years before the Anunnaki are
defeated at Armageddon in 2106 CE. As this is 460 years before the
Flood, it is exactly 5520 months. Historians have long recognized the
links between the ancient Maya and the Chinese. It is interesting that
this calendrical start of China is the 414th year of the Mayan Calendar,
or a Cursed Earth period.

2660 BCE (1235 AM): 4765 Before Armageddon/ 421 Before
Flood/ 2579 Nemesis Cataclysm/ 1649 Phoenix Year/ 1379
Capture of Luna/ 713 Olmec Calendar/ 155 Anno Pyramid

Cainan died at the age of 910, once a mighty Sethite king. Noah was
179 years old, his future wife Naamah was 261.

2653 BCE (1242 AM): 4758 Before Armageddon/ 414 Before
Flood/ 2586 Nemesis Cataclysm/ 1656 Phoenix Year/
1386 Capture of Luna/ 720 Olmec Calendar/ 460 Mayan
Calendar/ 186 Anunnaki Dynasty/ 162 Anno Pyramid

Planet Phoenix enters the inner system completing its 138-year orbit
and exits on its way back out to the Kuiper Belt. This is one Cursed
Earth period before the Flood (414 years) and this year uniquely
synchronizes with the Mayan Calendar. It is 460 years of the Mayan
Long-Count, or 5520 months (552x10). The other ancient American
system, the Olmec, has it at 720 years, or ten Precessional Years (72
years is one degree in the cycle of precession).

In studying pre-Flood histories of the Sumerians, Zecharia Sitchin found
a cataclysmic account described in the records that perfectly depicts a
Phoenix disaster. Sitchin's findings showed him that it occurred

- AFTER the appearance of the Anunna on earth (3439 BCE year of descent).
- BEFORE the Great Deluge (2239 BCE).
- When Nemesis X Object was STILL IN INNER SYSTEM (2707 BCE-2647 BCE).[1] This cataclysmic episode was admitted by Sitchin to be mysterious, but a record of it was found and the fragment was included in the narrative of his work.

NOTE: In the 138-year chronology of Phoenix, only ONE appearance fits all three of these chronographical parameters: 2653 BCE. Sumerian records reveal that the Anunna observed volcanic activity, quakes, fiery rocks from the sky, turmoil in the heavens, annoying dust storms, "demons" in space approaching the earth, and the *Moon under assault.* A celestial "Dragon of the Deep" *darkened the Sun* and cast the moon in shadow before the lunar body was covered in clouds from an impact. The Dragon (Phoenix) disappeared, the Sun returned, and *"...Nibiru to its distant abode in the Deep was returning."*[2] This Phoenix disaster occurred in Nemesis X Object's 54th year in the inner system, 6 years before Nemesis X Object exited the inner system, moving back toward Nemesis in the Deep (south of Sol). Nemesis X Object has NEVER darkened the Sun... this is the chief characteristic of Phoenix.

1. *The Lost Book of Enki p. 152-155; 2. Lost Book of Enki p. 152-155.*

2650 BCE (1245 AM):
Sumer was overrun by Semitic tribesman about this time.[1]

1. *A Global History of Man, p. 71.*

2647 BCE (1248 AM): 4752 Before Armageddon/ 408 Before Flood/ 2592 Nemesis Cataclysm/ 1662 Phoenix Year/ 1392 Capture of Luna/ 792 Anunna Arrival/ 456 Vedic Calendar/ 168 Anno Pyramid

After 60 years north of the ecliptic on its highly elliptical orbit, Nemesis X Object passes back through the inner system and completes its 792-year orbit. This is the 82nd year of the reign of the Nephilim king, Enmenluanna. Nemesis X Object's appearance in the inner system is calendrically significant. This is 2448+2448 months (408 years) before the Flood. The 2592 years of the Nemesis Cataclysm is 864x3. It has now been exactly 792 years since the Watchers descended in 3439 BCE. Noah is 192 years old, and his future wife Naamah is 274 years old.

Hurrians built Urkesh in North Syria just southeast of Turkey. Their language is still virtually undecipherable.[1]

Prof. Walter Emery claims that the Shemsu Hor was a master race over other cultures in ancient Egypt.[2]

Second Dynasty of Egypt, during time of Pharaoh Zoser (Djoser), builder of the stepped pyramid at Saqqara, which is dated about 2650 BCE.[3]

Ancient Chinese text, *Nei Ching* (translates to *Inner Canon* or *Inner Classic*), dates to 2650 BCE,[4] a book of medicine containing modern diagnoses and treatment plans. Attributed to the Yellow Emperor, said to have lived sometime between 2697 – 2597 BC, with book appearing (or reappearing) between 475 – 221 BC.

2647 BCE-2239 BCE, Tiahuanacu I.
2239 BCE-1899 BCE, Tiahuanacu II.
1899 BCE-1687 BCE, Tiahuanacu III.

To about 2500 BCE the Beaker People from Holland and the Rhineland moved into Britain, introducing metallurgy, dominating culture in Southern England.[5] They were a megalithic culture – people that would be powerful by 1800 BCE with a flourishing Bronze Age culture.[6]

2647-2239 BCE was a period of social deterioration, with a breakdown in race relations, wars, and rapid loss of technical, medical, and scientific knowledge.[7]

Minoan Linear A represented a Semitic language, coming from the shores of the Eastern Mediterranean. [8]

Ancient Greeks wrote that a Phoenician named Kadmus (ancient) brought them the alphabet.[9]

Aryan means "noble men," or "Lordly."[10]

Not only are titles, words and descriptions reversed by the later Greek renderings, but the following Canaanite/Phoenician and early Greek alphabetical symbols are all reversed in later Greek, as if imaged in a mirror: Alpha (A), Beta (B), Gamma (C, G), Epsilon (E), Vau (F, V), Iota (I), Kappa (K), Lambda (L), Mu (M), Nu (N), Pi (P), Rho (R), Sigma (S).

The transition from the older Semitic Alphabet to the post-Dorian Indo-European adoption of this alphabet reversed 13 letters, but the Delta Δ, Zeta I, Heta Ḥ (modern Eta E), Theta Θ, Xi …, Omicron O and Tau T, when reversed backward, remain the same letter, unchanged. After the Aryan Doric flood into the Aegean and Greece, the older Semitic and Egyptian traditions and texts were written down backward because Indo-European scribes wrote from left-to-right,with what was formerly, in the Mediterranean world, written only from right-to-left (Semitic). Sitchin dates the Minoan Civilization of Crete to circa 2700 BCE to 1400 BCE.[11]

Amorite civilization begun, one having venerated Sumerian gods.[12] Amorite names are listed in texts of Sumer and Akkad.[13]

Most pyramids in Egypt are within 50 miles of Cairo and the Giza Complex. Abu Roash, Saqqara, Dahshur and Meidum, and they date to circa 2685-2188 BCE officially,[14] but the real period is 2647-2239 BCE.

The Indus Valley cities were planned, with drainage and sewage systems laid out with carefully organized streets. Archeologist Mohammed Abdal Halim asserts that no cities of ancient Mesopotamia or Egypt exhibit evidence of such sophistication.[15]

Note: There is evidence that the Sumerian pre-Flood history was not in the Near East. There were no Sumerian cities as sophisticated as Harappan (the Indus Civilization) because Sumerians moved in 2239 BCE from Egypt to the Near East.

Archeologists estimate that the foundations of the earliest temples in Sumer were laid in early dynastic times, before 2700 BCE.[16]

Sumerian civilization began after this date but maintained historical records of the 792 years from the appearance of the Anunnaki in 3439 BC. Sumerians maintained schools, had homework, technical knowledge, and all the traits of high civilization acquired elsewhere, with historical memories not their own. Their rulers boasted of constructing canals, temples, and works of art. These rulers cherished the office of EN.SI, or righteous shepherd.[17] Sumerian culture was compassionate, and produced substantial poetry of love and lovemaking themes. Women in Sumer and Akkad of all walks of life had status and privileges unequalled until the 20th century, being prominent in business and property management.[18] In Sumerian art, women are depicted performing all sorts of functions and archeologists have found many female statues and figures.[19]

Sitchin acknowledges a mystery he cannot explain. Gold was mined extensively in antiquity for the Anunnaki, however, the archeological evidence show that at about 2500 BCE *"...gold came into royal use, indicating a change of attitudes whose reasons are yet to be explored."*[20] The reason is clear. In 2647 BCE the Anunna departed. Humans continued to mine gold and had no one to give it to. Sitchin again makes a metallurgical connection relating to departure of the Anunna and again he does not recognize the value of his own observation. In *The Lost Realms,* he notes that the Bronze Age of the Near East was in full swing from about 3500-2600 BCE (3439 BCE-2647 BCE being 792 years) when supplies of tin dwindled and almost petered out.[21] With the Anunna gone, tin mining in that entire hemisphere ceased, if it continued at all. It would be about 500 years before tin would be available again to make bronze. Shortly after the Great Flood in 2239 BCE, a Caucasian people moved into the Near East, establishing Bronze Age civilization.

The Indus Valley culture is believed to have begun *"...before 2500 BCE,"*[22] according to *A Global History of Man*. The city of Mohenjo-Daro was flooded more than once and rebuilt.[23]

The most unusual excavation of Mohenjo-Daro and Harappa have revealed the *"...shattered remains of an older culture of equally remarkable character, roughly datable from 3000 BCE, or slightly before, to about 2500 BCE."*[24] The Indus Valley civilization after the Deluge was rebuilt many centuries after a cataclysm that occurred before the Flood.

That the streets of Mohenjo-Daro were carefully oriented to the Sun[25] is proof of the Indus Valley civilization was founded after the Great Flood.

Mohenjo-Daro and Harappa are about 500 miles apart.[26]

Robert Temple in *The Sirius Mystery* found that the Celts, Greeks, ancient Chinese and Egyptians all highly regarded a 60-year period in antiquity. Learning from an old obscure book from 1827 CE written by George Higgins titled *The Celtic Druids*, Temple noted that Stonehenge and other British stone circles encoded a 60-year period.[27] Citing Chinese historian Dr. Herbert Chatley, he notes that the 60-year period venerated in early China found its origin in the *"...era of 2637 BC."*[28] While this dating is an approximate (era) attached to a definite (2637 BCE), it lies but ten years after 2647 BCE, when the Nemesis

X Object weapon exited the inner solar system. Plutarch wrote that the number 60 is the first of measures for such persons that concern themselves with the heavenly bodies.[29] The early Egyptians represented the 60-year period as a crocodile, an astronomical symbol. This vicious reptile is sacred in Egypt as a relic memory of the reptilian-amphibious Anunnaki, who walked among men for a period of 60 years on two separate occasions, several centuries apart. Temple's conclusion is startlingly accurate, writing that the link between the crocodile symbol and 60 years *"...probably echoes an earlier association of that cycle with the amphibious aliens."*[30]

The Mongols, Manchu, and other Tartars of Asia had cycles of 60 years, divided into five 12-year periods.[31]

This is the Exodus of Anunna, 792nd year, or 4896 months [2448+2448] before the Great Flood. After the Deluge in 2239 BCE, in the 792nd year afterward, the descendants of the Anunna, the Israelites (Amurru) would depart Egypt in a similar Exodus in 1447 BCE (2448 AM). 2647 BCE begins the Abandonment & Shock Period, which is 408 years to the Deluge.

2647 BCE began the Abandonment & Shock Period of 732 years of no Anunna contact with humans, to 1915 BCE.

Homo Anunna departed, leaving behind Caucasian Homo sapiens specialists who preserved the knowledge of sophisticated technolithic quarrying, transportation, and dressing of stone, but not their precision building techniques. Humans continued to use Anunna hardware that had been left behind. Perhaps the left-behind materials were not a concern to the Anunna, due to the known cataclysm soon to visit the world in 2239 BCE.

Shemsu Hor, or The Followers of Horus, according to Hancock and Bauval, followed after the reign of the gods in Egyptian prehistory. *"The Egyptians' own accounts also invite the conclusion that the role of these 'followers' may have been to carry down through the ages a body of extraordinary knowledge harking back to the even more mysterious 'Time of the Neteru' – i.e. the gods."*[32] Also, "From available primary sources, in other words, the overall picture that emerges is that the 'followers of Horus' may not have been 'kings' in the usual sense of the word but rather immensely powerful and enlightened individuals... at the sacred site of Heliopolis-Giza..."[33]

Shemsu Hor had the gift of knowledge.[34]

The earliest surviving references to the Followers of Horus occur in the Pyramid Texts.[35] Egyptologists conceded that these texts are merely transcripts of even older writings no longer extant. The scribes that copied them often *"...did not understand the words they were copying."*[36] Wallis E. Budge wrote, *"The Pyramid Texts are full of difficulties of every kind. The exact meanings of a large number of words found in them are unknown... the construction of the sentence often baffles all attempts to translate it... and contains wholly unknown words..."*[37] It is a mystery, with ancient Egypt's records being descended from a more advanced literature that preceded it. Hancock and Bauval wrote, *"These Followers of Horus bear with them a knowledge of Divine Origin."*[38] Egyptian traditions attribute the founding of Heliopolis to the Followers of Horus.[39] It would not have been called Heliopolis until after the Deluge, during the Heliolithic Period.

The *Turin Papyrus*: Here, after Horus, is listed the Shemsu Hor, called the Ancestors, or Sages, Ghosts (white), the Followers of Horus, a semi-divine race who *"...the Egyptians remembered as having bridged the gap between the time of the gods and the time of Menes."*[40] This was 749 years (7x7x7 years) to 1899 BCE (**2647-749= 1898 BCE**).

Shemsu Hor is also called the Akhu. They reigned 13,420 years.[41] Hancock nor Bauval, perhaps not wanting to address the obvious racial references, did mention that in the *Turin Papyrus,* the Followers of Horus were called, by the darker native Egyptians, *"ghosts,"* and this is significant. Ghosts are luminous, white, and the same description was given to Captain Cook and his English sailors when they made first contact with the Aborigines of Australia. Cook marveled that the Aborigines, in fear, averted their eyes and learned later that it was because the natives thought they were ghosts. They had never seen white-skinned people and Cook's party were thought to have been the dead, walking among them, so they maintained a respectful silence waiting for them to leave. That the Shemsu Hor were racial outsiders with bright skin, unlike the darker natives of the Nile valley, is proven in the title given to the Followers of Horus, called Akhu, meaning *shining ones*.[42] This was a racial description of Caucasian people given by a dark-skinned race. Throughout the annals and traditions of antiquity we find this over and over again – that non-Caucasian peoples perfectly described white-skinned visitors who appeared to them with a superior technology and knowledge of the sciences, but it has been misinterpreted over and over in *modern times* as the appearance of so-called *"gods"* or aliens on ancient earth.

Ignatius Donnelly in *Atlantis: The Antediluvian World*, wrote that the Indo-European (Caucasian/Aryan) center of government before the Flood was Sippara, known as the City of the Sun, according to Berossus.[43] This was the seat of the Noahian Children of the Sun. It was where the antediluvian records were buried in secure vaults to be retrieved after the disaster.[44] But the Sumerian city of Sippar is not the original site where arks were built and archives buried. No, the Shemsu Hor were of Egypt, a Caucasian race, called Children of the Sun *after the Flood*, and after the collapse of the vapor canopy (birth of the Sun). The Sumerians received disaster refugees in the form of a people far superior to themselves, and the naming of a settlement as Sippara was actually the borrowing from the original Saqqara of Egypt – just as the Greek colonies of Thebes and Abydos were originally places in Egypt, but brought to Europe by way of fleets.

The racial group referred to as the Children of the Sun began at Sippara, known as Sakkarah, in Egypt before the Flood. However, it was only after the Deluge that they were known by this appellation.

The oldest traditions of Khemet (pre-Dynastic Egypt) hold that it was a matriarchal goddess-worshipping culture.[45]

In Genesis 6:1-3 it states how the divine beings were attracted to the daughters of men and took them as wives. In Genesis 6:4 it states – "It was then, and later too [after that], that the Nephilim appeared on Earth—when the divine beings cohabited with the daughters of men, who bore them offspring. They were the heroes of old, the men of reknown."

Rob Skiba in *Archon Invasion* holds that the words, *"...after that,"* in Genesis 6:4 "...is a reference to something that occurred shortly after the events of Genesis 6:1-3 and entirely in a pre-Flood context." The synchronized, biblically-endorsed, extrabiblical texts become quite useful at this point in helping us to understand what is really being said here. Moreover, those texts lead us into an understanding that there was actually a *return of the Nephilim before the Flood.*[46] The *Jubilees* text reads that the Watchers descended in the 10th Jubilee (456 Annus Mundi is 3439 BCE) in the days of Jared, and descended again in the 25th Jubilee (1248 Annus Mundi is 2647 BCE). This rabbinical text dates the first and second descent perfectly with the 3439 BCE and 2647 BCE appearances of Nemesis X Object.

After the departure of Homo Anunna, their Caucasian descendants maintained the infrastructure of civilization from ANNU (later called Heliopolis/On) in Egypt. The Giza Complex was abandoned, sealed, declared a sanctuary, and guarded against disturbance. Additionally, groups of the Shemsu Hor traveled to distant regions building colonies. At this time, humans of all races priorly enslaved by the Anunna were productive in employing their various knowledge acquired under indenture to the construction of megalithic cities, quays, ports, canal works, fortifications, and terraced landscapes – all built using abandoned or stolen Anunna technology. A number of new cites, now world-famous, were begun in proximity of older technolithic architecture originally built by Homo Anunna. Examples are as follows.

- The enormous blocks of andesite lava in South America are articulated with such incredible precision with myriads of planes, indentations, grooves, and intricate keystone cuts that the conclusion is incontestable... these blocks are technolithic, machined to precision and could only have served a very specific mechanical function. One is reminded of the technolithic Grand Gallery of the Great Pyramid, with its obvious engineering function.
- Kashmir in Tibet: Megalithic ruins of a temple called Parshaspur, outside Srinagar, is a scene of total destruction. Huge blocks of stone are scattered about a wide area, exhibiting evidence of an intense explosion. The large dressed blocks are similar to the massive stone slabs of Puma Punku in South America,[47] identifying these ruins as technolithic.
- The Black Desert of Arabia: This covers an area of 100,000 square meters, once a city complex and about 5000 years old, with massive walls of basalt, ancient dams, and canals (but now in the middle of a desert). There are numerous petroglyphs of long-horned cattle and other domesticated animals. The city was built around 3000 BCE by the *"...Old Men of Arabia,"* an admission that the Arabians know nothing about it. One carving at Jawa depicts an acrobat vaulting over a long-horned bull in the same manner as found in the famous Minoan art of Knossus.[48] Known as Jawa, it once lied amidst fertile land, with huge herds of wild animals. The city is constructed of magnetized basalt.[49]

Will Hart, in *The Genesis Race*, wrote on page 104 concerning ancient South America, *"Grand scale architectural complexes emerged between 2700 BCE and 1800 BCE, corresponding to the building of ziggurats in Sumer and the Step Pyramid in Saqqara in Egypt."*

Will Hart wrote, *"Harappan civilization appears to have blossomed abruptly in an extraordinarily sophisticated form some time around 3000 BCE to 2500 BCE... complete with sewer systems, orderly streets, and public and private baths. Their racially mixed society – as depicted in their statuary and other artwork... included at least 1500 separate settlements."*[50] Tablets with inscriptions have been found but are undecipherable.[51] Hart notes that there is no evidence of armies, no temples, no palaces, colossal architecture, no displays of wealth.[52]

In the Indus Valley, Mohenjo-Daro, Dholavira, Lothal Mohenjo-Daro, and Harappa all seem to have sprung up fully planned.[53]

Indus Valley people of the Harappan cities were not Aryan.[54]

A statue on Mohenjo-Daro shows a man wearing a well-groomed, short beard.[55]

Sumerian records tell of two ancient sea-faring nations in the 3rd millennium BCE whom they traded with, called Makkan and Meluha, in the vicinity of India.[56] These probably being the Indus Valley civilization and the Dravidian culture of India, both having numerous port cities.

The Harappan script of the Indus Valley has a corresponding script on the other side of the world at Easter Island, or rongorongo script, which is still undeciphered.[57]

Lothal was excavated in 1954 CE. The archeologist S.R. Rao, who oversaw the digs wrote, *"The largest structure of baked bricks ever constructed by Harappans is the one laid bare at Lothal on the eastern margin of the township to serve as a dock for berthing ships and handling cargo... in no other port of the Bronze Age, early or late, has an artificial dock with water-locking arrangements been found. In fact, in India itself, hydraulic engineering made no further progress in post-Harappan times."*[58]

Lothal was a major port city of the Indus civilization, laid out in chessboard style like Mohenjo-Daro and Harappa, but now located far away from the Gulf waters. It has the same sophisticated drainage system, bathrooms, and fireplaces as other Indus cities.[59]

This 408 years to the Deluge (2239 BCE) was one of prosperity, peace, with international, transcontinental commerce and trade. It is evident from archeological findings that humans of all races multiplied into the many millions, that some Nephilim giant races also thrived, and cities were erected around the world. There is a dearth of evidence showing that battles or wars were fought in this period.

2647 BCE is 408 years to the Great Deluge in 2239 BCE, called the Sun of Water Fourth Age in the ancient Mexican histories, recorded in the *Codex Vaticanus*. The Four Ages of Man in the Vaticanus tradition start with *antediluvian* history.

In the *Codex Vaticanus* we find that the Aztecs count, as their start for the First Age, a period called The Water Sun. This is the beginning of their calendar, a year [said to be] 4008 years before the Great Deluge.[60] This 4008 is an obvious translator's error, either on the part of ancient Americans or the Spanish, for the correct amount of years was 408, from the 2647 BCE Nemesis X Object's pass, to the 2239 BCE Phoenix pass.

Some Sinologists believe that the Chinese culture originated in Mesopotamia.[61] In the Middle East, the Sumerian language stands alone for it is agglutinative, in this respect belonging to the same group as the Chinese.[62] Even today, the Chinese syllabary is based on signs fundamentally similar to the Old Sumerian pictographs.[63] In structure, proto-Sumerian resembles Chinese and Turkish, but in vocabulary, it resembles no known languages living or dead.[64]

The Mexican manuscript *Codex Vaticanus* (taken from the library where kept) relates the Four Ages of the World, preceding our own. Kingsborough wrote that the First Age was of giants who were destroyed by famine. The Second Age ended in a fire that burned the world. The Third Age was of monkeys. The Fourth Age is called the Sun of Water, a Great Flood, and the length of time is designated as 4008 years.[65] This 4008 years is inflated, either arbitrarily or by mistranslation, from 408 years, being from 2647 to 2239 BCE.

Egypt, Indus Valley and China are all aligned at 30 degrees latitude north of the equator, all three being pre-Flood civilizations.[66]

Will Hart wrote, *"Whenever we find civilizations with pyramids and the beginnings of irrigation agriculture, we find accounts of 'gods' descending to earth to teach humans how to live a civilized life."*[67]

Elamite civilization dates its beginning to approximately 3000 BCE, in southwest Iran.[68]

The Nazca lines of South America are of unknown provenance, antedating the jungle where they are found to pass under, stretching for hundreds of miles in straight lines from Nazca to even Tiahuanacu. An earlier civilization carved them out of the earth, and then another culture, later, maybe the Nazca, excavated them again around 100 CE.[69] Because the Nazca lines are of vast geometrical designs and artistic animal agriglyphs, only *seen from the air*, they could have been manufactured by humans who felt abandoned by the gods and attempted to induce their return. This idea is supported by the fact that Nazca lines are discovered extending all the way to Tiahuanacu, where the famous Gate of the Sun shows a human leader *crying tears* while offering up the symbols of kingship to 48 "gods" (winged figures) who have *ascended*. An equally plausible explanation, however, points to the creation of the Nazca lines during vapor canopy times, when the sky was not only reflective, like a mirror, but also magnified the heavens. In this case, one would not have to see these creations from above, but could stand there, looking up, to marvel at their amazing work without going anywhere.

E.LAM was name of the mountainous region east of Sumer.[70]

1. Before the Flood p. 178; 2. Elder Gods of Antiquity p. 195; 3. Elder Gods of Antiquity p. 215; 4. Ibid p. 216; 5. In Search of Ancient Astronomies p. 86; 6. Ibid p. 87; 7. The 12th Planet; 8. The 12th Planet p. 62; 9. Ibid p. 23; 10. Ibid p. 64; 11. The 12th Planet p. 62; 12. The 12th Planet p. 84; 13. Ibid p. 84; 14. Mysteries of the Ancient World p. 57; 15. Mysteries of the Ancient World p. 89; 16. When Time Began p. 142; 17. When Time Began p. 364; 18. Ibid p. 364-365; 19. Ibid p. 376; 20. The Lost Realms p. 231; 21. Ibid, p. 243; 22. A Global History of Man p. 63; 23. Ibid p. 63; 24. The Tigris Expedition p. 269; 25. Ibid p. 270; 26. Ibid p. 270; 27. The Sirius Mystery p. 377; 28. ibid p. 382; 29. ibid p. 383; 30. ibid p. 384; 31. Atlantis: The Antediluvian World p. 121; 32. The Message of the Sphinx p. 193; 33. The Message of the Sphinx p. 193; 34. The Message of the Sphinx p. 202; 35. The Message of the Sphinx p. 202; 36. ibid p. 345; 37. ibid p. 346; 38. ibid p. 213; 39. ibid p. 202; 40. The Message of the Sphinx p. 209; 41. The Message of the Sphinx p. 209; 42. The Mystery of the Sphinx p. 209; 43. Atlantis: The Antediluvian World p. 59; 44. Ibid p. 59; 45. Mushrooms and Mankind p. 51; 46. Archon Invasion p. 75; 47. Lost Cities and Ancient Mysteries of South America p. 272; 48. Lost Cities and Ancient Mysteries of Africa and Arabia p. 45; 49. ibid p. 46; 50. The Genesis Race p. 85; 51. The Genesis Race p. 85; 52. ibid p. 86; 53. Flying Serpents and Dragons p. 41; 54. Flying Serpents and Dragons p. 41; 55. Lost Cities of China, Central Asia and India, p. 227; 56. The Genesis Race p. 87; 57. The Genesis Race p. 27; 58. Lost Cities of Ancient Lemuria and the Pacific p. 82; 59. Lost Cities of China, Central Asia and India p. 186; 60. Atlantis in America p. 72; 61. Flying Serpents and Dragons p. 49; 62. ibid p. 49; 63. ibid. p. 49; 64. ibid p. 54; 65. Atlantis: The Antediluvian World p. 84; 66. The Genesis Race p. 90; 67. The Genesis Race p. 92; 68. Lost Cities of China, Central Asia and India p. 149; 69. Lost Cities and Ancient Mysteries of South America 25; 70. The Genesis Race p. 175.

2635 BCE (1260 AM): 4740 Before Armageddon/ 396 Before Flood/ 2604 Nemesis Cataclysm/ 1674 Phoenix Year/ 1404 Capture of Luna/ 204 Anunnaki Dynasty/ 180 Anno Pyramid

The *Ancient Earth-Killer* Comet Group passes through the inner system after 330 years below the ecliptic on its 396-year orbit. This is the 204th year of the Anunnaki Dynasty, or 2448 months. Enmenluanna has been ruling for 94 years.

2609 BCE (1286 AM): 4714 Before Armageddon/ 370 Before Flood/ 2630 Nemesis Cataclysm/ 1700 Phoenix Year/ 1430 Capture of Luna/ 504 Mayan Calendar/ 230 Anunnaki Dynasty/ 206 Anno Pyramid

The third king of the Nephilim Dynasty of the Anunnaki is Enmengalanna, another priest of heaven, of the metalworking city of Badtibira. Under his reign, the people began altering the natural order of nature. In this year, someone tunneled through the upper masonry of the Great Pyramid from the Descendant Passage into the Ascendant Passage system to survey stress fractures and damage caused by earthquakes. This tunnel is present today. Interestingly, this is 4714 years to the year 6000 AM (2106 CE). In the Annus Mundi year of 4714 (820 CE), the Arab Caliph of Baghdad, Al Ma'mun, tunneled into the Great Pyramid and discovered the Ascendant Passage's system. This is 504 of the Mayan Calendar, or 6048 months (864x7). As this was the 230th year of the Anunnaki Dynasty, it was 2760 months (552x5). This was the 300th year (108,000 days) since the Anunnaki matriarch emerged to rule in 2909 BCE. Noah is 230 years old. Enmengalanna will reign for 28,800 shars (evenings and mornings), or 80 years. The reign will end in 2529 BCE.

2569 BCE (1326 AM): **4674 Before Armageddon/ 330 Before Flood/ 2670 Nemesis Cataclysm/ 1740 Phoenix Year/ 1470 Capture of Luna/ 534 Vedic Calendar/ 270 Anunnaki Dynasty/ 246 Anno Pyramid**

At the exact midpoint of the 80-year reign of the Nephilim King Enmengalanna, the *Ancient Earth-Killer* Comet Group passes through the inner system, completing its 396-year orbit. The group spends 330 years below the ecliptic and 66 years above it.

2529 BCE (1366 AM): **4634 Before Armageddon/ 290 Before Flood/ 2710 Nemesis Cataclysm/ 1780 Phoenix Year/ 1510 Capture of Luna/ 910 Anunna Arrival/ 286 Anno Pyramid**

The fourth king of the Nephilim Dynasty, Dumuzi, begins to reign from the metalworker city of Badtibira. The ancient scribal and modern scholarly confusion between Dumuzi and Enoch is due to a chronological parallel involving Enoch's birth year of 622 Annus Mundi, and the year he was made Emperor, when chosen over 130 kings and princes in 3151 BCE. The early Sumerian chroniclers were aware that Enoch ascended into heaven and was born on the 622nd year of a pre-Flood calendar – however, because Dumuzi's reign began exactly 622 years after Enoch became Emperor in 3151 BCE, over time, the accounts of Enoch and Dumuzi were merged, making Dumuzi ascend into heaven as well. This year is 666 years after Seth had learned in 3195 BCE about the coming of the Flood. Noah is 310 years old at this time, this being the 300th year of the Nephilim Badtibira Dynasty.

2515 BCE (1380 AM): **4620 Before Armageddon/ 276 Before Flood/ 2724 Nemesis Cataclysm/ 1794 Phoenix Year/ 1524 Capture of Luna/ 324 Anunnaki Dynasty/ 300 Anno Pyramid**

Planet Phoenix passes through the inner solar system, completing its 138-year orbit and begins its journey back toward and into the distant Kuiper Belt. This is the 324th year of the Anunnaki Dynasty, 108x3 and 300 years (108,000 days) since the completion of the Great Pyramid in 2815 BCE.

2500 BCE (1395 AM):

Near Eastern Sumerian texts have been discovered claiming that the <u>average</u> yield on a field of barley was 86 times the sowing.[1] This was an exaggeration. The world benefitted from a vapor canopy that trapped greenhouse gases with increased carbon dioxide. The human population explosion must have been astonishing.

1. *A Global History of man p. 59.*

2473 BCE (1422 AM): 4578 Before Armageddon/ 234 Before Flood/ 2766 Nemesis Cataclysm/ 1836 Phoenix Year/ 1566 Capture of Luna/ 900 Olmec Calendar 630 Vedic Calendar/ 366 Anunnaki Dynasty/ 342 Anno Pyramid

The Priest Jared died at age 962, the father of Enoch. Enoch was given a vision of the chronology of the world, up until the appearance of God to gather His redeemed, a date revealed to him as being 5500 years after his 40th year, which was the year 500 Annus Mundi, signifying the year 2106 CE. Jared's death was 432 years (108x4) after the foundation of the Great Pyramid was laid in 2905 BCE. Noah was 366 years old. This was the 56th year of the reign of the Nephilim king Dumuzi.

2446 BCE (1449 AM): 4551 Before Armageddon/ 207 Before Flood/ 2793 Nemesis Cataclysm/ 1863 Phoenix Year/ 1593 Capture of Luna/ 369 Anno Pyramid

A five-planet alignment of Mercury, Venus, Mars, Jupiter, and Saturn was seen from Earth and recorded by the Chinese as occurring in this year, with the Emperor Chueni reigning.[1] This is exactly 207 years before the Great Flood, 207 being 2484 months (414x6), or half a Cursed Earth period of 414 years. This places this alignment of planets within the Phoenix Year, for 414 years is three 138-year Phoenix orbits. The Great Flood in 2239 BCE will be the 2070th year of the Phoenix Year, or 207x10. Whether a five-planet alignment occurred or not, this is further evidence that the ancient Chinese had access to accurate pre-Flood timelines. Noah was 393 years old at this time. This was the 83rd year of the reign of Dumuzi.

1. *The Great Pyramid: Its Divine Message 323-326 A. Tables XVII-XIX.*

2429 BCE (1466 AM): 4534 Before Armageddon/ 190 Before
    Flood/ 2810 Nemesis Cataclysm/ 1880 Phoenix Year/
    1610 Capture of Luna/ 684 Mayan Calendar/ 386 Anno
    Pyramid

This is the 400th year of the Badtibira Dynasty of metalworkers and
its last, ending with the reign of Dumuzi. The fifth Nephilim king
is Ensipazianna, who would reign for 28,800 shars (evenings and
mornings), or 80 years. This begins the Larak Dynasty, a city of giants.
This is 1296 years (108x12) after the start of the Sethite Dynasty in
3725 BCE. The Nemesis Cataclysm timeline is based on periods of
60 and 600 years, and we see this as true with the Anunnaki history
as well. 480 years before the Larak Dynasty was founded was 2909
BCE, when the Anunnaki matriarch founded her own dynasty over the
Canaanites. 480 years is 60x8. The Genesis record in chapter 6 related
that *"...and there were giants in the earth in those days,"* being the
offspring of the Anunnaki (angels) and human females. These were
called the Nephilim, meaning, The Fallen Ones. This new government
is reflected by the fact that this was 476 years after the foundation of
the Great Pyramid was built, the number 476 signifying a change in
government, that will be shown over and over throughout this research.
The Anunnaki moved kingship from Badtibira to Larak. This dynasty
of one king lasted 28,800 days=shars, or 80 years (360 days a year), to
2349 BCE.

2415 BCE (1480 AM): 4520 Before Armageddon/ 176 Before
    Flood/ 2824 Nemesis Cataclysm/ 1894 Phoenix Year/ 1624
    Capture of Luna/ 400 Anno Pyramid

This year is added to Chronicon because it figures very prominently
more than once in the chronometry of the Great Pyramid, a very
significant year. This was 490 years (70x7) from when the foundation
of the Great Pyramid was laid. It was the 424th year of the life of Noah.
This is also the 14th year of the reign of Ensipazianna of Larak.

2399 – 2300 BCE

<u>2377 BCE</u> (1518 AM): 4482 Before Armageddon/ 138 Before
   Flood/ 2862 Nemesis Cataclysm/ 1932 Phoenix Year/ 1662
   Capture of Luna/ 438 Anno Pyramid

Planet Phoenix passes through the inner solar system, completing its
138-year orbit on its way back out to the Kuiper Belt. This is its last
pass before appearing during the Great Flood.

<u>2359 BCE</u> (1536 AM): 4464 Before Armageddon/ 120 Before
   Flood/ 2880 Nemesis Cataclysm/ 1950 Phoenix Year/
   1680 Capture of Luna/ 1080 Anunna Arrival/ 744 Vedic
   Calendar/ 480 Anunnaki Dynasty/ 456 Anno Pyramid

Noah was 480 years old when he received a divine commission from
God to warn the people of the coming Flood, and to repent so that they
can be saved. The Great Flood is now <u>decreed</u> and the salvation being
offered is spiritual. God has determined to destroy Earth. Mankind is
given 120 years. At the Sumerian city of Shuruppak, Noah gathers
all the records of his forefathers, the secret writings of the Sethites,
including histories and prophecies, and preserves them. Noah is chosen
to survive the Flood, with his family, because he is perfect in his lineage,
meaning that he is 100% Sethite – therefore <u>Adamic</u>, with no Canaanite
or Nephilim influence in his bloodline, the latter being degenerate
hybrids not made in the image of God. The scriptural records on this
warning are in Genesis and Jasher.[1] The *Atrahasis* record indicates that
at this time, humanity filled the earth with their noise and corruption,
troubling the heavens.[2]

By this time, the Creator had severed communication between the
heavens and the rebellious Anunnaki. They were given <u>Phoenix</u> as a
sign and witness in the heavens of His plans, and on earth they were
given the Sphinx and Great Pyramid complex. But now, the Anunnaki
had to rely on <u>inspired humans</u> to know the times, to understand God's
plans because they had fallen from their first estate. This included the
prophets, the elect, and spiritually powerful, whom had to rely on for

<u>knowledge</u>. For this reason, Enoch was chosen and able to interact with the Anunnaki and Nephilim without harm. Though he pronounced judgements (from God) against them, he was their link to the Mind of God. Banished from the heavens by God, the Anunnaki also succeeded in banishing humanity from paradise and divine protection.

For this reason we see that the calendrics indicate that this flood warning, received by Noah and humanity, was also to the Anunnaki and their Nephilim offspring, a judgement decreed. This was 4464 years before Armageddon (2106 CE), a time when the Anunnaki will be defeated and confined by the Chief Cornerstone, the Stone they rejected. This 4464 years is 744x6. And this year (2359 BCE), the year Noah was warned, was the 744th year since the Vedic Calendar began – the Black Age caused by Anunnaki. This was the 480th year of the Oppression of the Sethites, or eight 60-year periods. The connection to Enoch was made more profound by the fact that this was the <u>792nd year</u> (orbit of Nemesis X Object) since Enoch was made Emperor in 3151 BCE, the year <u>744 Annus Mundi</u>. This was also the 70th year of the reign of the Nephilim king Ensipazianna.

The *Gilgamesh Epic* has the hero cut down 120 trees to build a boat to cross the river of death.[3] It is a sum identical to the 120 years found in Genesis, when Noah was warned of the coming flood and began building his boat.

Matsya Purana of Vedic literature has Manu as a heroic king, specifically, a Son of the Sun.[4] Manu was told by Vishnu that *"...the Great Deluge will be preceded by a universal conflagration which, following on a hundred years of drought and famine, shall consume the world."*[5] In Genesis, Noah was warned of the deluge 120 years in advance, a number borrowed from Sumero-Babylonian versions. In the Vedic version, the flood hero is given at least a 100 year warning.

In the *Shatapatha Brahmana* of India, the hero Manu is confronted by a fish (Oannes) that said, *"In such a year the Great Flood will come. Thou shalt attend to my advice by preparing a ship; and when the Flood has risen thou shalt enter into the ship, and I will save thee from it."*[6]

1. Genesis 6:3-4, Jasher 5:8-11, Flying Serpents and Dragons, p. 97; 2. Atrahasis p. 16-17; 3. Origin of Biblical Traditions p. 148; 4. Atlantis: The Antediluvian World p. 73; 5. Atlantis: The Antediluvian World p. 74; 6. Atlantis in America p. 174.

2357 BCE (1538 AM):

According to Chinese traditional history, in the *Book of Myriad Things*, the Emperor Yau ascended to the throne in this year, with some antiquarians claiming that this begins the historical period for ancient China.[1] This date is only <u>two years</u> off from the 120-year warning given to Noah in 2359 BCE, and further, the title "Yau" is akin to the ancient Semitic name for God: Yah/Jah. Noah, in the Sumerian records, was a king of the city of Shuruppak. Noah's story strongly links this Yau to being a Chinese Noah, since during the reign of Yau there occurred a terrible Flood.[2]

Ti-ku's son Yao ascends the throne of China, thus beginning the Historical Period.[3]

1. *Feats and Wisdom of the Ancients, p. 15; 2. Atlantis: The Antediluvian World p. 208-209;*
3. *Atlantis: The Antediluvian World p. 209.*

2349 BCE (1546 AM): 4454 Before Armageddon/ 110 Before Flood/ 2890 Nemesis Cataclysm/ 1960 Phoenix Year/ 1690 Capture of Luna/ 490 Anunnaki Dynasty/ 466 Anno Pyramid

The sixth king of the Nephilim Dynasty is Enmenduranna, who would reign 21,000 shars (evenings and mornings), or 58 years and 120 days. This ends the Larak Dynasty that lasted 80 years, and begins the Sippar Dynasty. Sippar is a metropolis and center of learning and science, housing a famous pre-Flood library that later Sumerians, after the Flood, would excavate. It is from these records that Noah retrieves the writings he is instructed to preserve. This is 490 years (70x7) since the founding of the Anunnaki Dynasty in 2839 BCE, and eight 70-year periods since the Anunnaki matriarch began to rule the Canaanites in 2909 BCE. This is the <u>480</u>th year of the Seven Kings of Sumer, who began to rule in 2829 BCE, the Nephilim Dynasty.

Anunna moved kingship from Larak to Sippar, a dynasty of one king, lasting 58.33 years (21,000 days on 360-day year) to 2290 BCE.

2341 BCE (1554 AM): 4446 Before Armageddon/ 102 Before Flood/ 2898 Nemesis Cataclysm/ 1968 Phoenix Year/ 1698 Capture of Luna/ 762 Vedic Calendar/ 474 Anno Pyramid

Noah married the daughter of Enoch, the prophet-Emperor. Her name is Naamah and she was 580 years old. She is stunningly beautiful and destined to be the oldest living person on Earth after the Flood, being

82 years Noah's senior.[1] Before the Flood, Naamah was chosen because she was the daughter of Enoch, being perfect in her lineage, but after the Flood Naamah would become infamous. Noah and Naamah's unions marked the beginning of the end for the Nephilim Dynasty offspring of the Anunnaki, and this is reflected in the Nemesis Cataclysm – the year being 2898, or 414x7, seven Cursed Earth periods. Further, the Vedic Calendar, also an Anunnaki timeline, has this as 762, the number for dynastic change. In this year, the human family has its <u>origin</u> through the Noahic and Enochian lines, both of Sethite ancestry, and purely Adamic. Noah is 498 years old.

1. Jasher 5:15-16.

2339 BCE (1556 AM): 4444 Before Armageddon/ 100 Before Flood/ 2900 Nemesis Cataclysm/ 1970 Phoenix Year/ 1700 Capture of Luna/ 1100 Anunna Arrival/ 774 Mayan Calendar/ 500 Anunnaki Dynasty/ 476 Anno Pyramid

Naamah gives birth to Japheth, the first-born son of Noah, 100 years before the Flood.[1] After Noah's death (after the Flood) Japheth will be the oldest male on Earth. The ancient Indo-Aryan peoples remembered Japheth as Pra-Japati and Iapetus, the origin for the Roman god Jupiter. Old Arabic traditions hold that the sexual maturity for a female before the Deluge was approximately at 200 years.[2] The world before the Flood is fully detailed in my book *Return of the Fallen Ones*. The biospheric conditions on Earth before the collapse of the marine water canopy in the sky (the biblical "firmament above") that caused the Flood were very different, and human longevity was not abbreviated as it is today. This explains the long, pre-flood lifespans documented in the Bible. Those pristine conditions, according to many ancient chroniclers, Josephus among them, lasted in the centuries, not decades. Before the Flood, people aged but did not physically grow any older in appearance. Once a man reached maturity, he remained physically in that form until death. The wrinkled skin and greying of the elderly that we experience today was not known to the ancients.

This year was the 476th year since the Great Pyramid was complete. As will be seen throughout this research, the number 476 is found over and over throughout the duration of all timelines dealing with the descendants of Japheth, even after the Semitic lines from Shem merge with the lineage. This number signifies a change in government. This is the 490th year (70x7) of the Nephilim Dynasty, founded in 2829 BCE. This is the 90th year of the reign of Enmenduranna, or 1080 months.

1. Genesis 5:32, Jasher 5:17; 2. Tales of the Prophets, p. 92.

2338 BCE (1557 AM): 4443 Before Armageddon/ 99 Before Flood/ 2901 Nemesis Cataclysm/ 1971 Capture of Luna/ 477 Anno Pyramid

Naamah gives birth to Ham 99 years before the Flood,[1] Noah's second son. He will be remembered in antiquity as Chem, Chemmis, Amon, Ammon, Hamma, Hammon, Anom, Anam, and Am. He is the patriarch of the Hamitic line, peoples that populated Egypt, Africa, Australia, parts of India and Cambodia, and also Central America, who were known anciently as the Olmec.

1. Jasher 7:1.

2337 BCE (1558 AM): 4442 Before Armageddon/ 98 Before Flood/ 2902 Nemesis Cataclysm/ 1972 Phoenix Year/ 1702 Capture of Luna/ 776 Mayan Calendar/ 478 Anno Pyramid

Naamah gives birth to Shem 98 years before the Flood,[1] Noah's third son. Shem is the 11th in descent of the Ten Patriarchs of the Adamic lineage, through Seth, these being the unpolluted generations not contaminated with Canaanite or Nephilim influence. Shem would be the patriarch of the Semitic branches of humanity that would preserve the Scarlet Thread (Holy bloodline) through Abraham, Isaac, Jacob, and the 13 Tribes of Israel who would merge with the Japhetic lines, and become major nations and empires. This is 776 of the Mayan Calendar, the number 776 throughout history exhibiting the union between Japhetic and Semitic people, as prophesied by Noah in Genesis.

1. Jasher 7:1, 5:18, Genesis 11:10.

2335 BCE (1560 AM): 4440 Before Armageddon/ 96 Before Flood/ 2904 Nemesis Cataclysm/ 1974 Phoenix Year/ 1704 Capture of Luna/ 1104 Anunna Arrival/ 504 Anunnaki Dynasty/ 480 Anno Pyramid

The Sumerian King List records that Etana (Enoch) ruled for 1560 years before the Flood, but this is a chronological mistake. The duration of pre-Flood history from Man's Banishment in 3895 BCE was 1656 years (414x4), but the 1560 discrepancy derived from the fact that 1560 is <u>130 months</u>, and Enoch ruled over 130 kings and princes. The Sumerian scribes erred – however, this date does indeed appear to be significant to the Anunnaki. It is 1104 years (552+552) after the Anunnaki descended to earth in 3439 BCE, and 504 years (6048 months is 864x7) after the Anunnaki Dynasty began.

2325 BCE **(1570 AM): 4430 Before Armageddon/ 86 Before Flood/ 2914 Nemesis Cataclysm/ 1984 Phoenix Year/ 1714 Capture of Luna/ 1114 Anunna Arrival/ 490 Anno Pyramid**
Egyptian priest-historian Manetho of Alexandria wrote that ten rulers after Thoth (Enoch) reigned 1570 years until a very chaotic period when government and historical records ceased (Great Flood). This is a fragment concerning the pre-Flood world's Ten Patriarchs, with the same story being remembered in Plato's narrative about the ten kings of Atlantis. This old Egyptian 1570 year period is similar in duration to the Sumerian King List's 1560 years.

2313 BCE **(1582 AM): 4418 Before Armageddon/ 74 Before Flood/ 2926 Nemesis Cataclysm/ 1996 Phoenix Year/ 1726 Capture of Luna/ 800 Mayan Calendar/ 502 Anno Pyramid**
The second Mayan baktun completes here (288,000 days) from the start of the Mayan Calendar in 3113 BCE, being 800 years. This is 888 months to the Great Flood (74 years), with 888 being a Golden Proportion number.

2309 BCE **(1586 AM): 4414 Before Armageddon/ 70 Before Flood/ 2930 Nemesis Cataclysm/ 2000 Phoenix Year/ 1730 Capture of Luna/ 506 Anno Pyramid**
This was the 600th year since 2909 BCE, when the Anunnaki matriarch established her rule over the Canaanites, and 520 years (52x10) after the Nephilim sons of this matriarch established their own dynasty over the Sethites, these seven called the Seven Kings. This is the 40th year

of the reign of Enmenduranna of Sippar, the sixth king of the Nephilim Dynasty. This year begins both the Giant Wars and the Antediluvian Apocalypse. A plague afflicts the world and the earth is teeming with humans and hybrids. The Nephilim progeny of the Anunnaki, the hybrid giants, are discontented with the state of the empire, believing that the millions of humans are responsible for the food shortage. The Anunnaki hybridization programs had created races of gigantic people too numerous to be controlled. The giants multiplied, but the Anunnaki did not. Just as the Anunnaki rebelled against their Father, the Eternal One, so too did their own sons, the Nephilim, rebel against them. The Apocalypse occurred during the reign of the Seven Kings, before the Flood, just as a similar Apocalypse would again transpire during the reign of Seven Kings (Nephilim overlords) in the future (21ˢᵗ century CE). Many among the giants turned to cannibalism, and humans were now a food source.

Sitchin wrote that the final seven <u>shars</u> before the Flood was a period of drought, famine, and pestilence.[1] His mistaken interpretation of 3600 years to a shar (attributed to Berossus and corrected by many scholars today) means this devastating period lasted 25,200 years, a totally untenable idea. Seven shars of <u>3600 days</u> each is <u>70 pre-Flood years</u> (3600=10 years x7).

Wilkins in *Mysteries of Ancient South America*, on page 88 wrote, *"It is a disturbing coincidence that ancient myths stress that the catastrophes [the coming Flood] of thousands of years ago were preceded by gigantic wars, and that men wandered forth, warning of the wrath to come, of which these wars were the premonitions."*

1. *The 12ᵗʰ Planet p. 400-401.*

2299 – 2239 BCE

2297 BCE (1598 AM): 4402 Before Armageddon/ 58 Before Flood
2297 BCE is a variant dating for the Chinese Flood of Yao. It is 58 years off from 2239 BCE.[1]

1. *Secret Cities of Old South America*, p. 376.

2291 BCE (1604 AM): 4396 Before Armageddon/ 52 Before
    Flood/ 2948 Nemesis Cataclysm/ 2018 Phoenix Year/ 1748
    Capture of Luna/ 524 Anno Pyramid
The Seventh king of the Nephilim Dynasty of the Seven Kings is Ubarutu of Shurrupak, a city that Noah had lived in. Ubarutu would reign 18,600 shars (evenings and mornings), or 51 years and 240 days, to the Great Flood in 2239 BCE. The 240 days of Ubarutu's reign, added the 120 days of his predecessor's reign, completes the final year, 360 days. Ubarutu's reign would be *"cut off"* by the Deluge, which involved planet Phoenix in 2239 BCE – but as the Seventh King, he may reappear in the 21st century CE, in the Apocalypse, in 2052 CE, as described in the Revelation account where the Eighth King, is of the Seven.
In the year 2046 CE, the Nemesis X Object will nearly collide into earth and alter its orbit around the Sun during an invasion of Anunnaki, with the Revelation text stating that a third of the day and night would be reduced because Earth's spin rate is increased. This means that our 365-day year in the future, after 2046 CE, would become 240 days. Interestingly, the ancient Persians believed that the historic time before the Flood saw the rulership of the Abad Dynasty, which was known for avarice, murder, vice, and the total collapse of civilization.[1] This perfectly reflects the Revelation account, which calls this Seventh King ABADdon. He is the Destroyer. This date is 52 years before the Flood.

1. *Round Towers of Atlantis*, p. 246.

2290 BCE (1605 AM):
Anunna moved kingship from Sippar to Shuruppak, a dynasty of one king lasting 51.66 years (18,600 days), to the Great Flood in 2239 BCE.

2283 BCE (1612 AM): 4388 Before Armageddon/ 44 Before Flood/ 2956 Nemesis Cataclysm/ 2026 Phoenix Year/ 1756 Capture of Luna/ 532 Anno Pyramid
The ancient record on the golden tablets translated for King Phillipus in 498 BCE claim that in this year, these texts, upon the tablets, were copied from the surfaces of the Great Pyramid to be preserved for future posterity after the Flood.[1] This is consistent with other traditions about Noah preserving records. Many references among old writings have claimed that the surfaces of the pyramids at Giza were covered in texts. This was the 556th year of Noah, the 54th year of Shem.

1. The Origin and Significance of the Great Pyramid, p. 112-114.

2281 BCE (1614 AM): 4386 Before Armageddon/ 42 Before Flood/ 2958 Nemesis Cataclysm/ 2028 Phoenix Year/ 1758 Capture of Luna/ 558 Anunnaki Dynasty/ 534 Anno Pyramid
The Anunnaki homeworld Nemesis X Object reaches aphelion far out in the Kuiper Belt, the furthest distance it travels from the Sun. It was last in the inner system 366 years priorly in 2647 BCE, and now begins its 366-year journey back toward the inner system, below the ecliptic.

2254 BCE (1641 AM):
This is the traditional date for the Chinese Flood, in which Fu-Hi (Noah) survived.[1] This demonstrates that the Chinese knew that Fu-Hi lived for hundreds of years, for they believed him to have been born in 2944 BCE. The Chinese date is only 15 years off from *Chronicon's* flood date of 2239 BCE, and we find here evidence that the ancient Chinese were aware of planet Phoenix, which initiated the Flood disaster. They ascribe a life to Fu-Hi of 690 years (2944-2254 BCE), 690 being five orbits of Phoenix at 138 years each.

Fuh-hi was succeeded by Shin-nung, who reigned 140 years. He introduced agriculture and medicinal science.[2]

1. The Great Pyramid: Its Divine Message, p. 285; 2. Atlantis: The Antediluvian World, p. 208.

2246 BCE (1649 AM): 4351 Before Armageddon/ 7 Before Flood
In the *Atrahasis Epic*, we learn that a seven-year famine became so severe that cannibalism occurred.[1] This is supported in a very old tablet dated 28th day of Shebat, the 11th year of Ammi-zaduga, located today in the Pierpont Morgan Library Collection. A Babylonian document, it concerns the Great Flood and refers to a dire famine that preceded it. Albert T. Clay wrote that this old deluge account was of Amorite composition.[2] It states that it was itself a copy of a much older document. It is interesting that in the apocalyptic Book of Revelation, a famine occurs before the Phoenix disaster (Sixth Seal) and flooding (Trumpet Judgement). Atrahasis was Noah's personal name before the Deluge; the title he was known by, after the cataclysm, was Utnapishtim.[3]

1. *Atrahasis p. 14; 2. Origin of Biblical Traditions p. 146-147; 3. Origin of Biblical Traditions p. 166-168.*

2244 BCE (1651 AM): 4349 Before Armageddon/ 5 Before Flood/ 2995 Nemesis Cataclysm/ 2065 Phoenix Year/ 1795 Capture of Luna/ 571 Anno Pyramid
Lamech, father of Noah, dies at age 777.[1] Many righteous people still holding to the Elder Faith began dying, with the Creator allowing for the demise of those that believed in Him in those days before the Deluge so that *"...they should not see the evil which He had declared to come."*[2] Noah chose the three daughters of Eliakim (the son of Methuselah, who is the son of Enoch), to marry his three sons, Japheth, Shem and Ham. These were Enoch's granddaughters, and Noah was married to Naamah, Enoch's daughter.[3] Because of escalating violence, Noah moved his family to a place appointed in the wilderness to escape the giants (Nephilim).[4] God instructs him on the design of a massive wooden structure, designed to float – that being a ship, and Noah begins the five year long project.[5]
Noah is commanded to make the ark the length of *"...three hundred cubits, the breadth of fifty cubits and height of thirty cubits."*[6] The architectural dimensions of the Ark are no different than those of the Great Pyramid, encoding chronometrical timelines relative to mankind. The ancient Royal Cubit equals 20 Pyramid Inches, each Pyramid Inch being a year within the chronometrical timelines. Thus, 300 cubits is 6000 years, the duration between Man's Banishment, in 3895 BCE,

and his redemption in 2106 CE. The width of the ark at 50 cubits was 1000 Pyramid Inches, a millennium, exactly one/sixth the length of the Ark, with 6 being the number of Man. The height of the structure at 30 cubits was 600 Pyramid Inches, a Great Year, or Anunnaki NER, the age of Noah when the Flood occurred. The Great Pyramid is the height of a 40-story building, at 5448 Pyramid Inches, or 454 Pyramid Feet. But the Ark is 6000 Pyramid Inches longer, and if stood on end it would be 552 inches higher than the Great Pyramid. The Flood occurs at the end of a 552-year cycle in the Phoenix Year, and the Subterranean Chamber width under the Great Pyramid is 552 inches. The Ark had three decks and was so spacious that it could carry the loads of 500 railroad boxcars.

Noah is remembered as the Sumerian Utnapishtim, Zusuthrus of Babylon, Manu of ancient India in Sanskrit and Vedic texts, Bochica of early America, Deucalion of Greece (New Wine Sailor), Nereus in the Aegean, Fu-Hi of China, and Coxcox in Mexico.

1. Genesis 5:31; 2. Jasher 4:20; 3. Jasher 5:34-35; 4. Josephus, Antiquities Book I; 5. Jasher 5:34; 6. Genesis 6:14-15.

2239 BCE (1656 AM): 4344 Before Armageddon/ 3000 Nemesis Cataclysm/ 2070 Phoenix Year/ 1800 Capture of Luna/ 1200 Anunna Arrival/ 864 Vedic Calendar/ 600 Anunnaki Dynasty/ 576 Anno Pyramid

This is the year of the Great Flood, an event remembered by EVERY culture on this planet. There has been recorded over a thousand flood traditions and their similarities are stunning. The oldest Mesopotamian tablet inscriptions found, the Kharsag Tablets, describe the Flood.[1] Hebrew and Jewish traditions relate that the Deluge occurred in the 1656th year of the pre-Flood calendar, as we see here in the Annus Mundi dating. Augustine, over 16 centuries ago, wrote that the Flood occurred in the year 1656.[2] This sum, 1656, is 12 orbits of planet Phoenix at 138 years each, or 4 Cursed Earth periods at 414 years each. 1656 is also 3 Phoenix Cycles of 552 years each. The Flood disaster is mentioned famously by Pindar,[3] Ovid of Rome,[4] Lucian,[5] and Apollodorus,[6] among many others. The Chinese believed that the Great Flood actually marked and caused a major division in time itself.[7] The calendrics for this terrible year bear this out.

This is the 3000th year of the Nemesis Cataclysm timeline, a year when judgement is executed against them and their Nephilim offspring, which are killed off the face of the Earth. 3000 years is 5 Great Years of 600 years. This was the 2070th year since the destruction of the pre-Adamic World, or 15 orbits of Phoenix at 138 years each, 414x5 years. Since Earth entered its new orbit around the Sun in 4039 BCE, it had been 1800 years, or 600x3. From 3439 BCE, when the Anunnaki descended to Earth at the passing over of the Nemesis X Object, it had been 1200 years, or 600x2 (432,000 days). This was 600 years after the reign of the Seven Kings began, being the Anunnaki Dynasty over the Sethites. Thus, Noah was 600 years old and his wife Naamah, 682. The Anunnaki matriarch began her rule over the Canaanites 670 years earlier, in 2909 BCE, and the Sethites laid the foundation for the Great Pyramid, which was designed to survive the Deluge 666 years earlier, in 2905 BCE.

The Giza Complex was finished 576 years (144x4) before the Flood. The Black Age of the Kali Yuga, having begun in 3103 BCE, saw the rise of the Nephilim powers of the Anunnaki and decay of spirituality. The Flood <u>ended</u> the total presence of Anunnaki and Nephilim hybrids on Earth, as the Flood cleansed the planet of their pollution, reflected in that the Deluge was the year 864 (Foundation of Time number, implying a <u>beginning</u>) of the Vedic Calendar.

Seven days before the Deluge, planet Phoenix was seen entering the inner solar system, growing larger and larger in the sky from the direction of Venus. Phoenix transited between Earth and the Sun, casting our planet in shadow, <u>darkening the Sun</u>. The world turned upside down, night turned to day and day to night, and destructive earthquakes shook the foundations (crustal plates) of the world.[8] The Tractate *Sanhedrin 108b* reads that seven days before the Flood, the Sun set in the east and rose in the west and the *Book of Enoch* also mentions a pole shift and quakes at the Flood.[9] The Babylonian records, called the *Atrahasis Epic*, reads that, *"For seven days and seven nights the torrent, storm and flood came on."*[10] In the Persian *Zend Avesta* texts, the flood was associated with the sudden appearance of a strange <u>star</u>.[11]

Before the seven days began, Noah had loaded the Ark with all the necessary water and provisions. The ancient *Book of Jasher* relates that the Creator caused animals of mammalian, and some avian species as well, to gather around the superstructure, and they allowed Noah and his sons to take their cubs and young ones into the pens of the Ark. Noah had just finished collecting the pups and cubs and livestock when *people* began gathering around the Ark. He shut his family inside of it, and as it began raining, about 700,000 people surrounded the Ark. But the people were refused admittance and rioted when Noah reminded them of the years of his preaching and prophesying, which they had ignored. The masses of enraged and panicked men and women assaulted the structure in what became the Battle of the Ark. The *Jasher* records indicate that God enraged the hearts of the animals that had delivered their young, and thousands of wild animals set upon the rioting people.[12] Mighty men (giants, Nephilim), vicious women, and angry men fought to enter the Ark but the sons of Noah from atop the structure fought them valiantly, with the animals and the people fighting one another. The storms increased and they fled to find shelter.

Sumerian records attest that just prior to the 40 days of nonstop rain the entire world shook violently and the far horizon turned black with clouds.[13] Rabbinical records indicate that the Deluge was caused by the falling of <u>two stars</u>.[14] These two impacts mirror what is described in the Revelation account during the Apocalypse (see 2046 CE and 2048 CE). Phoenix transits between Venus and the Earth, which led to much ancient confusion. We have records from archaic chroniclers that they thought Venus was responsible for the catastrophies that all occur with the Phoenix orbit years. These will be seen in 1687 BCE. The meteoric impacts that caused the Flood were not fragments from Phoenix, which merely blankets the Earth in millions of tons of cosmic dust, darkening the Sun in an envelope, but from the *Ancient Earth-Killer* Comet Group. This comet group fractured off the Nemesis X Object and entered its own orbit of the Sun of 396 years (half of Nemesis X Object's orbit), which just finished its 330 years below the ecliptic on its elliptical orbit. Now it begins its 66-year (792 month) journey over the ecliptic. As the past is a predicate for the future, the Sun's darkening from Phoenix precedes the impact of two gigantic meteoric objects, just as described in the prophetic biblical records.

An analysis of Chinese traditions using royal chronologies places Emperor Shun in <u>2240 BCE</u> (one year off from 2239 BCE) witnessing a large meteorite falling from the sky to strike the earth, followed by the Great Flood.[15] In 1998 CE, W. Bruce Masse, an environmental archeologist with the U.S. Air Force, revealed that the ancient world was plagued by a series of cosmic impacts, with one being approximately 2240 BCE.[16] Ocean sediments taken from the Gulf of Oman revealed a sudden deterioration of a long-stable climate in approximately 2200 BCE.[17] French scientists in the Middle East discovered layers of calcite under the ground indicating a cosmic impact dating around 2200 BCE.[18] Earthquakes and strange electrical storms rage as the heavens seem to spin end over end as Earth rolls without axial stability. Noxious gases and chemicals poison the world, killing many. The basement rock (foundations of earth) are broken and the entire surface of the crust is rippled with new mountains and valleys, and cities of the world are buried in violent subsidence. Pillars of lava are thrust high into the air as boiling water spews up from below the ground, appearing as towering geysers that flood thousands and thousands of square miles. Volcanic resurfacing occurs and the rains continue through it all. The marine atmosphere, a thick water vapor canopy that made the biospheric conditions of pre-Flood earth so unique, collapses. The source of the rainwater that caused the Flood was never terrestrial. In fact, the planet enjoyed a surface sea or seas, along with a literal ocean above, called in Genesis "the firmament." The firmament magnified the heavens like a lens, allowing the ancients a better view of the heavens, to see the planets closer up. In fact, the planets Venus, Jupiter, and Saturn still have these vapor canopies.[19] Had not a large celestial body penetrated the upper mesosphere at the exact same time that Phoenix exerted a powerful gravitational pull on Earth's outer atmospheric levels at the instant of direct transit between Earth and the Sun, the marine mesosphere would still be in place, and the stars and planets of the night sky would appear much larger. The Great Flood was the first time mankind had ever experienced rain. Rain was never necessary in the antediluvian biosphere because the mesosphere and subterranean water table, according to Genesis 2, caused a mist to water the face of the earth every morning and evening, through condensation. The mesosphere took 40 days to fall completely to the Earth. With internal core pressure intensified by the proximity of Phoenix, which is several times the mass of Earth, the subterranean water reservoirs boiled upward over the land at the same time the mesosphere drained the atmosphere of its watery firmament. The waters of the Flood are still with us today, having accumulated at the poles covering Antarctica in a two-mile high icecap, and at the North Pole. Some of it has mixed in with earth's oceans and precipitation cycle, but Antarctica still has 6.4 million cubic miles of ice which, if melted, would result in the oceans rising 190 feet worldwide.

Every time it rains on earth some of these water molecules are the same that had fallen out of the sky in 2239 BCE.

One of the greatest asteroid impacts on Earth was that of the Chicxulub Crater (120 miles in diameter and 19 miles deep) that carved out the bowl of the Gulf of Mexico – an impact zone that happened on the opposite side of the world from where pre-Flood civilization was centered in the land we call Egypt today. The Chicxulub event is said by scientists to have wiped out the dinosaurs about 65 million years ago and is located in the "Devil's Tail" area in the Yucatan of Central America. The prehistoric "Age of the Dinosaurs," however, was not 65 million years ago. The scientific testing of radioactive materials and their decay-rates does not take into account the contamination of radioactivity that occurred in 4309, 2239 BCE, and other disasters of interplanetary origin.

The Anunnaki, having taken on physical bodies that they cannot escape out of now, are imprisoned by the Godhead, those having descended to sexually unite with the daughters of men. Their progeny, the Nephilim, hybrids and giants, are obliterated from the face of the earth. The scribe of Jeremiah the prophet, named Baruch, wrote in what is now called *The Apocalypse of Baruch*, *"These were the Giants, famous from the beginning, that were of so great stature, and so expert in war. Those did not the Lord choose, neither gave He the way of knowledge unto them: but they were drowned because they had no wisdom, and perished through their own foolishness."*[20]

A global ocean is created and the Ark is lifted in the waters, megalithic anchor stones keeping it from listing. The former surface layers of the planet are scrambled and much is reconstituted according to weight and density, with billions of dead people, Nephilim hybrids, giants, and animals from land and sea are deposited in the deepening water and buried. Immense pressure from radioactive materials boil the oceans and entomb dead bodies in many layers. The saturated, carcass-strewn sediments are cooked under these conditions, which burned the effects of the Flood into the fictitious geologic column. The Old World has been turned into a planetary fossil of a former global ecosystem that had not known arctic poles nor seasonal changes, but was a virtual year-round greenhouse. A Babylonian record reads, *"...all mankind was turned to mud."*[21] The whole world was destroyed exactly 2070 years (414x5) after it was totally destroyed and frozen in 4309 BCE. The two planetary cataclysms and their sedimentation effects have given rise to the fiction of the Jurassic fantasy of millions of years ago. Prior to the Great Flood, the planet was more spherical than it is today. The crust of the planet was not fractured into plates as it is today. The Earth was literally <u>broken</u> at the Flood and the equatorial bulge was formed from the immense stress and pressure. The 7920-mile diameter of the planet became 7925 miles and the planet no longer spun around a perfect 90° axis as do the other planets closer to the Sun. Earth's axis became tilted at 23° inclined toward the ecliptic (despite the uniformitarianist claim that it happened 4.5 *billion* years ago). Intriguingly, this 23° tilt reflects the history of the Earth's precessional motion. Because the retrogression of the precession of the equinox is 1 degree every 72 years, in the year 2239 BCE (1656 AM) the Earth has gone backward, a total of 23° (1656 years), since Man's Banishment from paradise in 3895 BCE. The tilt of the earth now supports the maintenance of the polar caps and is the reason the world experiences seasonal changes, a fact unknown to the pre-Flood greenhouse.

The Genesis record of the Great Flood provides us another source of proof that the years in the antediluvian world were reckoned at 360 days. We are told therein that the Flood lasted five months and that these five months were 150 days.[22] This reveals a 30-day month, 12 of which would be a year (360 days).

More amazing archeological and scientific proof of the Deluge will be found throughout this research.

Each Yuga (Age) lasts 3000 years.[23]

Graeco-Roman chronographer Alexander Polyhistor in the 1st century BCE wrote that in the *2nd Book of Berossus*, the dynastic line before the flood lasted for <u>120 years</u>, which he claims was <u>432,000 years</u>.[24] Polyhistor wrote that this dynastic line had Ten Kings, confusing 10 shars of 120 years each for <u>1200 years</u> with Ten Genesis Patriarchs.

Sumerian fragment of the Deluge reads, *"For <u>seven days</u> and seven nights the flood swept over the land."*[25]

"On the <u>7th day</u> after this the three worlds shall sink beneath the ocean... thou shalt embark on the great ship."[26]

In the *Bhagavata Purana*, we read, *"In the course of <u>seven days</u> the ocean overflowed, and the earth was submerged by continual rain."*[27]

The Peruvian tradition of a Great Flood states, *"...the Sun was hidden by <u>a great darkness</u>."*[28]

In antiquity, it was said that the Sun <u>had been born</u> on or by the Great Flood.[29] This is reference to the <u>Fours Suns</u> of antiquity – the Phoenix transits of 2239 BCE, 1687 BCE, 1135 BCE, and 583 BCE.

At Dunhuang in the Gobi Desert in 1911 was discovered a cache of ancient texts written in a hitherto unknown <u>Aryan</u> language called Tocharish, [along with] some texts written in unknown language.[30]

<u>Baal</u> Hills in Yorkshire, England.[31]

The second destruction of Prydian (Briton) was by <u>fire</u>, the third by <u>drought</u>.[32]

In the <u>Edda</u>, in *The Sybil's Vision*, we find, *"<u>The Sun darkens</u>, earth in ocean sinks, fall from heaven the bright stars... towering fire plays against heaven itself."*[33]

<u>Ogyges</u> was King of Boeotia, according to Pausanias.[34]

<u>Ogyges</u> is claimed to have been a <u>son of Neptune</u> (Poseidon), related to the Titans.[35] But this would identify Ogyges as one who came from <u>the sea</u>. Ogyges was actually the son of Inachus, not Neptune. Inachus was a river god (not from the sea), and one of the Potamoi, which is what all the sons of Oceanus and Tethys were called. Oceanus, as grandfather, was also not a god of the ocean. He was a Titan, and the god of "the great encircling river Oceanus, believed to be the source of all fresh water on earth." When one understands the vapor canopy, it becomes clear that the lineage of Ogyges had nothing to do with the ocean.

Ogyges arrived during the reign of Phoroneus the Argive, son of Inachus, grandson of Oceanus and Tethys, progenitors of the Pelasgians, or <u>men of the sea</u>[36] (according to Acusilaus). Inachus was the Titan <u>Anak</u>, son of Oceanus or some attribute Arba of Argos.

Arba is listed in Joshua 14:15 and 15:13 in the cataloguing of the Giants as the father of Anak (Inachus), the giant forefather of the Anakim. My research links Anak of the Old Testament to Inachus of the ancient

Greek traditions – traditions which remember Anak also as Anax. Robert Graves also links the Anakim of Palestine to the Anax. Ogyges (son of Inachus) is described as gigantic by the root of his name, but he plays no part in history until his name is used for the Ogygian Deluge of 1687 BCE.

Ogygia was the island of the nymph Calypso, according to Homer.[37] Destroyed in the cataclysm, the name for this island serves as the root word in Apo(calypso).

From 2239-1899 BCE, groups of Indo-European people emerged from the Caucasus region, some migrating into northern India to become the Aryans (noble men).[38] Another wave migrated into Europe. A third wave moved into Anatolia, and came to be called the Hittites.[39]

Abydenus, citing Berossus, wrote, *"Kronos revealed to Sisithros that there would be a Deluge on the fifteenth day of Daisios."* Sitchin asserts this to be the second month.[40] New Year's being March 21, the vernal equinox, and the Flood occurred May 15.

Sitchin notes that Sisithros is merely Atrahasis reversed.[41]

Sitchin's misinterpretation of the 432,000 periods from descent of the Anunnaki to the Great Deluge shoved the timing of his Sumerian events to the impossible period of 428,000 years ago, causing him to search for data from the equally unsupported evolutionary-establishment dating of geological events. Following on relative dating methods, circular reasoning, and preposterous theories, Sitchin ignored hundreds of chronological citations from antiquity that would have unified the elements of his theory into a cohesive model of earth history.

Sitchin believed that the Great Flood referred to the last Ice Age,[42] a position in defiance of all the chronologies of the ancient world.

In the *Atrahasis Epic* it states that the moon disappeared…the Deluge set out… the darkness was dense. The Sun could not be seen.[43]

At Ashur, an Akkadian text with a profusion of Sumerian words was found and published by Dr. Erich Ebeling. Sitchin believed it refers to NIBURU (Nemesis X Object). *"His weapon is the Deluge; God whose weapon brings death to the wicked…the Sun, his God, he frightens… this is the name of the Lord who from the second month to the month Addar the waters had summoned forth…"*[44]

Sitchin claims that NIBURU at the Flood was called SHUL.PA.KUN.E,[45] which is close to the earliest title in Egypt for Phoenix (The PIN-God).

NIBURU never darkens the Sun, but with SHUL.PA.KUN.E, *"...the Sun, his God, he frightens."* Phoenix caused the Flood in May (second month from the New Year vernal equinox). NIBURU's weapon is the Phoenix planet/super construction, for their orbits are commensurate. Phoenix appears in the inner solar system in 2653 BCE, followed in 6 years by NIBURU (Nemesis X Object) in 2647 BCE, both Phoenix and NIBURU (Nemesis X Object) pass through in 522 CE. Phoenix appears again in 2040 CE, followed once again six years later by NIBURU (Nemesis X Object) in 2046 CE. Phoenix is the weapon of the Anunnaki Homeworld, known to the Anunnaki who *predicted* the Deluge and the Phoenix is their programmed technology.

Ebeling's Akkadian text, based off an earlier Sumerian record continues, *"Lord whose shining crown with terror is laden. Supreme planet a seat he has set up facing the confined orbit of the red planet. Daily within the Lion he is afire..."*[46] Sitchin attributes everything to NIBURU (Nemesis X Object). The *"Lord whose shining crown,"* is NIBURU, the *"supreme planet."* But the *"seat"* NIBURU has set up is a throne, a new orbit ruled by a red planet (Phoenix) that, with the Flood, has shown itself first as coming from Leo.

The Harappan port of Lothal was destroyed in the flooding (estimated-2200 BCE).[47] It was totally rebuilt.[48]

That Berossus cannot be trusted with measurement translations is exemplified in that he wrote that the ship (Ark) was 3000 feet long and more than 1200 feet wide,[49] a ridiculous size almost three times the length of the longest aircraft carrier in the world. Berossus somehow added zeroes to 360 feet long and 120 feet wide. The Flood was at the 3000th year of the Nemesis Cataclysm timeline, and the 1200th year of the Anunna Arrival.

The Jews in Babylon were perplexed over the two different Great Flood accounts in the Mesopotamian histories (3439 BCE and 2239 BCE) so much they included both versions in the Genesis narrative to describe the Flood of Noah. Genesis 8:13-14 specifically states that the Flood lasted for a period of one year and eleven days (360+11=371 days). But Genesis 7:12 reads that it rained for 40 days and 40 nights, Noah then sending out four birds at intervals of three successive periods of seven days. (Genesis 8:6-12) After a total of 61 days from the beginning of the Flood, Noah found the ground dry.

Why two accounts? Are these calculations true historically? One of them is a fabrication, shown in that 371+61=432, a perfect golden section sum found in many ancient texts and exactly one-thousandth of the 432,000 days (1200 years) from the first flood in 3439 BCE and the Deluge of Noah in 2239 BCE. The discrepancy is exasperated even further by Genesis 8:2-3, which asserts that the waters of the Flood did not decrease until 150 days had passed, which contradicts both earlier accounts.

Scholars have been perplexed as to why in the Sumerian-Mesopotamian pantheon, the Sun-god Shamash was depicted as the son of the moon god, Sin. Sitchin theorizes this was because the lunar calendar preceded the solar methods.[50] The real reason was the collapse of the vapor canopy – the "birth" of the Sun.

The epic struggle of Osiris and Set is heavily draped in mythological garbage. Set is associated over and over again with Typhon, or the Phoenix, which caused the Great Flood. In the myth, Lower Egypt was allotted to Osiris. Seth, Lord over Upper Egypt, trapped him in a chest, the sarcophagus in the Kings Chamber of the Great Pyramid, which was then cast into the Mediterranean. Osiris was drowned.[51] Osiris was associated to Lower Egypt and its drowning by the Mediterranean. That Set was the cause demonstrates the ancient Egyptian identity of Set as Typhon, or the Phoenix, the cause of disasters. The resurrection of Osiris in the legend was coupled with another miracle, the birth of his son, Horus.[52] Horus symbolized the birth of the Sun. In the *Chester Beatty Papyrus No. 1*, the appearance of Horus astounded the assembled gods.[53] Horus fought Set in the skies over the Sinai Peninsula.[54] This is an allusion to the Sun (Horus) appearing after the collapse of the vapor canopy.

Inca legends hold that the Sun, moon and stars did not appear until after a great flood caused by Viracocha.[55] It was said that after this flood the Sun appeared.[56]

The Toltec sky god was *Smoking Mirror* (Tezcatlipoca),[57] a corrupted memory of the vapor canopy.

In 2239 BCE and 1687 BCE, Posnanski concluded that there had been 3 phases of history at Tiahuanacu, and that in the first, Tiahuanacu was settled by a Mongoloid race but then a flooding disaster occurred. The second race to establish Tiahuanacu was a Middle Eastern Caucasian race, before a sudden, unknown upheaval of nature occurred, bringing a second cataclysm.[58] (see 1687 BCE)

From 2239 BCE to 1889 BCE (350 years) Manetho wrote that there was no ruler over the whole of Egypt.[59]

The Great Deluge brought about a major religious change among its survivors. Stellar deities and pantheons of Gods from the Deep fell out of favor as the post-diluvial peoples, after collapse of the vapor canopy, now began to worship the Solar Disk, and the lunar orb, which reinforced the antediluvian veneration of the Goddess.

A Sumerian Flood account published by Samuel Noah Kramer reads that Utu (the Sun-God) came forth shedding light on heaven and earth after, *"...the flood swept over the land."*[60] Utu is not an older Sumerian god like AN, ENLIL, or ENKI, but is introduced after the Diluvian disaster because they only appeared in the sky after the vapor canopy collapsed.

At the foot of the Pyramid Ziggurat of Nippur, archeologists found a library of 35,000 inscribed tablets, one containing the Sumerian version of the Great Flood. This oldest flood account mentions no mountain that survivors landed on (like Noah's Ark), but instead reads that after the flood mankind first settled in Dilmun. Later the Gods led them to their present location of Sumer.[61] The Deluge raged for seven days and seven nights and was over when Utu, the Sun God, came forth.[62] The Sumerian Noah, called Ziusudra, then prostrated himself to the Sun God, sacrificing an ox and a sheep.[63] This was the first appearance of Utu in the Sumerian pantheon and Ziusudra worshipped him because the disaster of the vapor canopy – collapsing and raining down to flood the earth – seemed to be over. There was the arrival of a bright new Sun, which before the Flood was hidden by the vapor canopy. So important was the Sun's appearance that in another account, the Flood Hero was named Utu-nipishtim.[64]

Heyerdahl wrote, *"...there was some major geological catastrophe in the Atlantic in a period late enough to coincide with an identifiable stir among all known early civilizations. Its worst effects must have been of the founders of the island cultures around Britain, as the disturbance formed a lasting split in the Atlantic Ocean floor..."*[65]

Egyptologists have their own special brand of world chronology totally divorced from any historical periods outside Egypt. However,

Egyptologists claim that <u>after</u> the Giza Pyramids were built, a collapse of Egyptian civilization occurred that they date as occurring at approximately 2200 BCE. This decay and ruin has been termed the <u>first Intermediate period</u>.[66] This is an inadvertent way to admit what they will not admit.

Astronomer and mathematician George F. Dodwell studied the observations of Manilius, Hipparchus, Thales, Pythagoras, Eratosthenes, Eudoxus, Pytheas, and Hindu and Chinese sources, to conclude that at 2345 BCE (a sine curve estimate) a major alteration in the <u>tilt of the Earth</u> occurred.[67] His estimate is 106 years before the flood. In the *Book of Enoch*, we read that before the flood Noah saw that the Earth *"had become inclined."*

"In the six hundredth year of Noah's life, in the second month, on the seventeenth day of the month, on that very day all the fountains of the great Deep were broken open, and the windows of the heavens were opened." (Gen, 7:11) Alexander Heidel notes that some scholars believe that the *"second month,"* is the second spring month, called Ziw and Iyyar, which *"corresponds to the latter part of April and early part of May."*[68] Thus, the 17th day of Iyyar, which begins in late April, gives us a date of <u>May 14</u> or <u>May 15</u> for the Great Deluge.

Sitchin notes that the knowledge of the coming cataclysm (Phoenix) was not given to humanity in general, only to the direct descendants of Enki. As will be shown hereafter, the knowledge of Phoenix was only in the possession of Caucasian people. Its timing was weaponized to invoke fear in enemy hosts, when Caucasian military operations were planned in advance of a Phoenix appearance.

Sitchin paints a picture of Anunna fleeing earth in spacecraft, horrified at having to abandon humanity to such a fate (the coming cataclysm). The problem with this scenario is the dearth of evidence showing that by this date (in the Post-Technolithic Period, or Abandonment & Shock Period) leading up to 2239 BCE, there were no Anunna with technological ships intact or even present. The last documented presence of Anunna/Anunnaki was in their mass exodus in 2647 BCE due to the cataclysm and appearance of Nemesis X Object. There is actually more evidence of the Anunna vanishing into underground facilities and whole multi-level subterranean cities than with anyone ever departing this world for the skies. Immense underground cities have been found by the dozens in Turkey, the first being excavated in 1962 CE. Others have been found in South America and another kept very secret in the Grand Canyon of North America, among others.

The *Matsya Purana* account holds that the Deluge occurs at the *end of an age*, a Yuga. This Aryan version is different from the Chaldean account that tells that the world was destroyed due to mankind's sin.[69]

In the *Bhagavata Purana*, we find, *"On the seventh day after this the three worlds shall sink beneath the ocean."*[70]

In Iranian (Persian) tradition, Yima, father of the human race, was warned by Ahuramazda that the world was about to be devastated by a Flood. The deity ordered Yima to construct an enclosure and stock it with seed, beasts, domesticated animals, and men. When the Flood occurred, the Garden of Yima was spared.[71]

There are more than 500 flood myths belonging to more than 250 different cultures and peoples.[72] In many of these traditions the world is burned before it is flooded.[73]

The Sumerian *Epic of Gilgamesh* reads that destruction came *at the appointed time...* a black cloud came out of the horizon that turned all that was light into darkness, *"...so that no man could see his fellow." "The tempest raged for six days and on the seventh it ceased."*[74]

The *Mayan Dresden Codex* shows a serpent-like dragon destroying the world by spewing water from the heavens, a draconic body adorned in *star constellations and eclipse symbols.* This serpent dragon was the Phoenix disaster personified when the polestar Alpha Draconis fell, the axis then pointing to a new pole star, Polaris in Ursa Minor. Beneath the eclipse symbols in this codex is the Old Woman Goddess, patroness of death and destruction, holding a *bowl from which a flood pours.*[75] The high antiquity of the symbols and motifs used in the Book of Revelation concerning the future Last Days apocalyptic events is seen here in the ancient American concept of floods causing ruination by the pouring of a bowl... being the Bowls of Wrath and flooding, also found in Revelation.

The Mayan book *Chilam Balam*, preserved in the Maya language (translated to Latin), reads of a fiery rain that fell with ash. Trees fell and rocks crashed about. The Great Snake was torn from the sky (pole star A. Draconis) and pieces of it fell to the earth (Phoenix fallout). *"Then the waters rose in a terrible flood. And with the Great Snake the sky fell in and the dry land sank into the sea."*[76]

A Sumerian text of the city Nippur dated about 1700 BCE reads that King Ziusudra was blessed with long life, like a god (longevity) and he *"...protected the seed of mankind at the time of the destruction."*[77]
Hopi traditions of ancient America maintain that Pahana, the White Brother, commanded a large fleet of boats filled with family and friends to escape the Great Flood.[78]
The Old Testament Genesis flood account, as shown by Albert T. Clay is actually, *"...two different and originally independent accounts of the Deluge which are combined into one."*[79]
There is an Egyptian legend of Sekhmet, the Mistress of Flame. She is called the Eye of Ra and is depicted in art with a lion head and the body of a woman – linking her to the Sphinx. The people of earth thought the Sun was too old (possibly considered weak, could not be seen), and Ra sought to exterminate humanity. The Eye of Ra, Sekhmet, was unleashed and earth became a burning wasteland. Ra released a liquid to stop the conflagration. Ra consulted with Geb and said that humans had survived in caves but their enemies, the snakes, were also underground. Ra promised to give mankind knowledge of words of power to exercise dominion over the snakes.[80] The age of the Sun, a deity attacking mankind, and an Eye in the sky (Phoenix), with a great burning of lands, are all familiar.
The "liquid" released by Ra was a flood and, following this catastrophe, writing was introduced into Egypt. This Sekhmet story is from the indigenous population of North Africans living a Neolithic life along the banks of the Nile long after the civilized builders of Giza, Abydos, and other sites departed about a thousand years earlier. The North African plate was lowered into the Mediterranean for 340 years, from 2239 to 1899 BCE. This story is older than the start of the Second Egypt, which would begin with the arrival of Menes and his people in 1898 BCE.
During the Macedonian Greek era the Babylonian priest-historian Berossus, concerning the Great Deluge and quoting older sources, wrote, *"...to him [Sisithrus] the deity Kronus foretold that on the 15th day of the month of Desius there would be a deluge of rain."*[81]
Genesis 7:4 reads, *"For after seven days I will cause it to rain on earth forty days and forty nights."*

In Egyptian Theban tradition, the Eight Builder Gods, the Ogdoad, identified the flood hero Noah as one of their own. Two titles that were given for one of the Ogdoad builder gods was The Far Distant and the Sailor.[82] These were very old titles for the Flood Hero. In Sumer, the hero of the Deluge was Utnapishtim, called The Far Away, and the earliest Greeks called him Deucalion, or New Wine Sailor.

Jim Marrs in *Our Occulted History* (2013) wrote, *"Scattered archeological excavation over many years indicate that what is regarded as the Great Flood was a planetwide catastrophe, though not every portion of the world went underwater... the kinds of conditions we might expect from a large planetary body passing by the earth."*[83]

Ivar Zapp and George Erikson in 1998 wrote that the near-miss of a large astronomical body would first set the sky on fire, initiating high winds. The intense heat at high altitude would result in a lower surface level loss of oxygen – hundreds of millions of life forms would have suffocated.[84] This was the fate of the megafauna, to suffocate, to be torn and tossed about by gales and then to float in bloated masses in a flood, in tangled heaps, in topsoil and permafrost.

Ovid wrote that many escaped the flood only to die of starvation afterward.[85]

The *Dresden Codex* of the Maya reads, *"The sky approached the earth and in one day all perished. Even the mountains disappeared under the water."*[86]

Nereus, the Old Man of the Sea, was a pre-Greek Peloponnesian memory of Noah, the name NEReus is simply the Anunnaki NER (600) personified. He is represented as fish-tailed like Oannes because he was a civilization savior after a flood. Hesiod (800 BCE) wrote that Nereus was trusting, gentle, and a teacher of the laws of righteousness.[87]

Occult histories derived from India inform us that the great Deluge interrupted a great world conflict, possibly a race war. After the Flood, it was the agenda of the forces of darkness to promote divisiveness between races. *"The seeds of hate and of separation have been fostered ever since that time, and the three modes whereby the forces of darkness seek to control humanity, are hatred, aggression and separateness."*[88]

It seems there is evidence for divisiveness, hatred, or even a race war at the Great Deluge, which has continued in many ways to this day.

François Lenormant said, *"...the Diluvian tradition is not primitive, but imported in America."*[89] Also, *"...it [the Flood story] undoubtedly wears the aspect of an importation among the rare populations of the Yellow Race where it is found."*[90]

Continuing, he states, *"...the story of the Deluge [is] a universal tradition among all branches of the human race, with the one exception, however, of the black..."*[91] Lenormant also wrote that the story of the Flood belonged to *"...the most ancient times,"* and was the history of Aryan, or Indo-European, Semitic peoples having *"descended from Noah."*

Berossus wrote that the Deluge occurred in the 18th SAR of the reign of King Xisuthros, he being warned by Cronus (the God of Time) *"...that upon the 15th day of the month Daesius there would be a Flood."*[92]

Lenormant in 1857 wrote, *"It is a very remarkable fact that we find in America traditions of the Deluge coming infinitely nearer to that of the Bible and the Chaldean religion than among any people of the Old World."*[93]

Ancient pre-Columbian Mexican traditions tell of a flood survivor, Coxcox, and his wife Xochiquetzal, living through the disaster in a boat. Paintings of them have been found in ruins of the Aztecs, Mixtecs, and Zapotecs, among others.[94]

The alarming uniformity of transatlantic deluge stories is disturbing. People witnessing the same event do not recall the same details in the same ways. The particulars of the Flood accounts are too exact – precise parallels are found on continents separated by oceans among people speaking different languages. The parallels are so precise on a global scale that the serious antiquarian can only conclude that the story of the Great Flood destroying all humanity, save a man and a woman in a ship full of animals and family members, was a specific story *spread around the world* in a syllabus by a mariner-missionary culture after the actual event. The synchronicities between flood versions in opposite hemispheres could never have resulted from individual memories. The story that we have passed down in all its variant veins was one that was *taught* over a long period of time to the unlettered, Neolithic peoples after coming in contact with civilizers.

The Flood occurred in the reign of Yau of China. This would have been the 118th year of Yau. This is not unreasonable in the Chinese chronology, that has Shin-nung reigning 164 years and Fu-hi 140 years.[95]

The Chinese Flood tradition reads, *"The pillars of heaven were broken; the earth shook to its very foundations; the heavens sunk lower toward the north; the Sun, the moon, and the stars changed their motions; the earth fell to pieces, and the waters enclosed within its bosom burst forth with violence... the Sun was eclipsed, the planets altered their course... "*[96]

A black cloud assailed the land of the Adites, out of which proceeded a watery storm.[97]

The Koran Surah LXIX.II states, *"And we caused the earth to break forth with springs... and the earth's surface boiled up. "*[98]

In Genesis, the human race that was drowned in the Deluge was called the Haadam.[99] The Adamu, the most populous race of men, however, did not represent all of the branches of human stock.

Hindu legend mentions Satarvata, who is told to secure the sacred books of the time in a safe place before the Flood.[100]

The Mandan Indians of North America hold that the world is a great tortoise, covered with earth (the crust covered in soils) and that long ago, a tribe of white men came and dug holes in the earth to great depth, piercing the tortoise shell, causing the waters to overflow and kill the men, save one who survived in a boat.[101] The man had a dove on the boat like Noah, and the digging is primitive memories of extensive mining operations. To describe the crust of the earth as a turtle shell is a barbarous gloss over a sophisticated understanding of our world.

Ignatius Donnelly wrote, *"The world might relapse into barbarism... but the memory of the cataclysm in which the center of a universal empire instantaneously went down to death would never be forgotten; it would survive in fragments, more or less complete, in every land on earth; it would outlive the memory of a thousand lesser convulsions of nature; it would survive dynasties, nations, creeds, and languages; it would never be forgotten while man continued to inhabit the face of the globe. "*[102]

Lucian wrote that Deucalion was the Noah of the Greek world. He asserts that the Greeks claimed that, *"The present race of men, they allege, is not the first, for they totally perished, but a second generation, who, being descended from Deucalion, increased to a great multitude. "*[103]

Lucian, on the Flood according to the Greeks, wrote, *"On a sudden [event] the earth poured forth a vast quantity of water, great rains fell, the rivers overflowed, and the sea rose to a prodigious height. All things became water, and all men were destroyed. Only Deucalion was left, for a second race of men...* "[104]

John Denham Parsons wrote, *"It is noteworthy that the ancient Egyptians, with all their knowledge of the past, and despite their acquaintance with the version current among the Greeks [Pindar, Ovid, Lucian, Apollodorus] and no doubt with the older if not original one of the Babylonians, had no such tradition. At any rate, Manetho declared that his countrymen knew of no such deluge."* [105]

In 1895 CE, John Denham Parsons wrote that the Flood occurred in the 600th year of Noah's life, *"...that is, at the meeting point of two of those famous cycles of six hundred years so often referred to by ancient writers. This cycle of six hundred years was often spoken of as the Great Year."* [106] This *"...six hundred year cycle to which so much importance was attached in bygone ages."* [107]

A cardinal belief of the Mexicans was that eternity had been broken up into cycles, the various epochs in which were marked by the destruction of successive Suns.[108] The world *"...had been destroyed by a great deluge... the old Suns were dead, and the present Sun was no more immortal than they."* [109]

The Inca version of the Great Flood recorded between 1570 CE-1584 CE by Cristóbal de Molina at Cuzco reads that, *"In the life of Manco Capac, who was the first Inca, and from whom they began to be called the Children of the Sun... they had a full account of the deluge. They say that all people and all created things perished in it, insomuch that the water rose above all the highest mountains in the world. No living things survived, except a man and a woman, who remained in a box... the wind carried them to Huanaco."* [110] Manco is a memory of the Vedic Manu and the Hebrew *Menahem* (Noah's name), who was the first of the Children of the Sun. The Flood account was not Incan, but an importation brought to them by others.

An ancient Zoroastrian belief held that the Original Creation was a time period lasting 3000 years.[111] This was the first of the Four World Periods.[112] Further, Plutarch, quoting Theopompus (4th century BCE), wrote that the Magi of Persia taught that the gods conquer each other every 3000 years.[113]

The oldest version of the *Atrahasis Epic* contains no evidence that it was written in the Sumerian language. In fact, not only does the Akkadian preserve Amorite words left untranslated, but the gods and heroes and many words in the narratives are Amorite.[114] Albert T. Clay wrote that the Flood story of *Atrahasis* was *"...mainly an Amorite legend which the Semites from Amurru brought with them from the west."*[115]

The collapse of the vapor canopy removed the barrier of protection that obscured the blinding light of the Sun – thus, the Sun was "born." The Birth of the Sun is a very old concept intrinsically attached in lore with the end of an age.

Lewis Spence in 1924 summed up the tradition in the Maya Quiche *Popul Vuh* text, writing, *"We have here a vivid description of the approach of a mighty flood, the descent of a fiery volcanic rain, the destruction of dwellings, the crashing of trees, and the ultimate plight of the wretched survivors, reduced to the condition of forest-dwellers."*[116]

Brenton in *Myths of the New World*, on page 245, cites 35 American tribes and relates that it is *"many others,"* as well, who all remembered a Great Flood, writing, *"There are no more common heirlooms in the traditional lore of the Red Race."*[117]

It is a peculiar element of the American flood traditions that the survivor is always the First Man.[118] The Adam of native America.

The *Codex Chimalpopoca* written in Nahuatl of Mexico reads, *"And this year was that of CeCalli [Kali] and on the first day all was lost. The mountain itself was submerged in the water, and the water itself remained tranquil for fifty-two springs..."*[119] This describes the submergence of the Great Pyramid at Giza beneath the Mediterranean, for a long time, or 52 springs, meaning a lengthy period. The Codex continues with a god who warns Nata and Nena of the coming flood and instructs them to make a boat out of a large cypress tree.[120] The association to Kali cannot be understated, for in the Old World Kali was the goddess of destruction and cataclysm, and the Kali Yuga Age ended with the Deluge. Both India and ancient America were early on influenced by white-skinned foreigners that had ventured into their interiors.

The Aztecs believed that the earth had been destroyed on several occasions – by the agency of fire, of tempest, and of water. They believed that the various *"suns,"* as they called the epochs of their history, had each been terminated by some awful convulsion of nature.[121]

"The Mexicans believed that the earth was not destined to receive its present inhabitants, although occupied by manlike beings, until it had undergone a series of cataclysms or partial destructions. "[122] This infers that the Aztecs believed themselves to be more human than pre-cataclysm mankind.

Codex Vaticanus of the Aztec tradition holds that in the First Age, or Sun, water reigned until at last it destroyed the world, an age that lasted 4008 years until the great deluge changed men into men-fish.[123] This 4008 years represents an exaggeration commonly used in reporting Egyptian time periods when zeroes were arbitrarily added in their narratives to provide great antiquity where none existed. This 4008 is actually 408 years, a time period that ended with the Flood in 2239 BCE and started in 2647 BCE when Nemesis X Object was in the inner system. 408 years is 4896 months, or 2448+2448 and, incidentally, the number associated to cataclysm in ancient Egypt was 2448.

Ixtlilxóchitl, in his *History of the Chichimecs*, called the First Age the Water Sun because it ended in a great inundation.[124]

Paralleling the Deucalion tradition, the Macusi tribe of the Arawak Indians believed that a survivor of the Flood repopulated the world by changing stones into human beings.[125]

The Tamanacs of Central America recall a man and woman surviving the Flood and casting behind them the fruits of the Mauritius palm tree, producing men and women.[126]

Spence wrote that in the oldest records of the Near East, *"...the presumption is strong that the Deluge legend dates from a time anterior to the occupation of the country by the Semites. "*[127]

The *Popul Vuh* claims that it was cloudy and twilight, that the face of the Sun and moon were covered.[128]

The collapse of the vapor canopy is evidenced by the fact that it was the first time humans witnessed a rainbow (as reported in the Bible), a prismatic effect that could not occur before.

Antediluvian climate was stable, it was a sub-tropical temperate world. In Genesis, which is a text of the Jews borrowing elements from Babylonian ideas, the Flood is brought on by man's depravity. In Sumerian texts, the Flood is brought on by the gods.

Isaiah 30:26 states that the world is engulfed in bright light seven days before the Flood.

The seven stars of the Pleiades were setting in May when the Flood occurred, these stars are ever afterward linked to *death and destruction*.[129] In Amos 5:8 we find, *"He who made the Pleiades and Orion, and brought on the shadow of death in the morning, and darkened the day into night, who calls for the waters of the sea and pours them out on the surface of the earth..."*

Wilkins, in *Mysteries of Ancient South America*, wrote on page 10, *"In the skies of terrible night shone a giant comet, or aerolite, or wandering star, or planet (we do not know which), but which brought such destruction on the earth that those who survived the disasters regained sanity only slowly, and in some cases, never."*

Wilkins continues, *"...The light of the Sun appeared to have gone out... for many days, indeed, night and day could hardly be told apart... the Sun hung like a ball of blood, but the penumbra soon darkened all the air, as in time of eclipse. Then, an immense cloud of reddish powder filled the air... when the pall of smoke had partly cleared, two moons [rode] in the sky..."*[130]

Aboriginal Indians of Brazil who took refuge on high summits to escape the Flood reported that terrible rumblings occurred in the sky and underground. The Sun and stars turned red, *"...a whole month passed and our forefathers heard a roar and saw darkness ascending from the earth to the sky."*[131]

The *Codex Chimalpopoca*, containing the history of the kingdoms of Culhuacan and ancient Mexico tells us, *"The sky drew near the water and, in a savage day all was lost. The mountains themselves sank underwater... Nata and his wife Nena escaped in a hollow cypress tree..."*[132]

The *Popul Vuh* of the Quiche (Maya) reads, *"The earth darkened and it rained night and day. Thus was accomplished the ruin of the race of man which was given up to destruction."*[133]

Ancient Mexican tradition preserves a curious detail, *"Those who came from the east beyond the sea could not cause the savages of the land to work or worship, and so there came a great deluge."*[134] This parallels the Sumerian versions of antediluvian history concerning the Anunna ruling over dark races that were subject to them. The Flood was caused due to the rebelliousness of mankind, as the story goes, and served as a control mechanism to induce the populace to behave or such an event would occur again.

"The Washoan Indians on the eastern slopes of the Sierra Nevada, who speak a language very different from other California Indians, have traditions about foreign invaders landing from the sea long ago and making them into a form of slave. These invaders appeared to have been survivors from some great cataclysm; for, says the myth, they made the ancestors of the Washoans pile up stones for a great temple whereon these '...*great lords might take refuge.*' It also appears that a great deluge rushed in from the sea, before this temple or Babel-tower had been erected, and drowned many of the Washoans and their conquerors."[135] It states, in this account, that "many" of the Washoans and their conquerors were drowned, but not all – so the survivors, wherever they went, added to the various flood traditions we have throughout the world. Many of the flood stories, being so similar, were part of a mariner syllabus shared with all peoples that these mariners, after the Flood, came in contact with.

Ancient Chinese legends recount a Great Flood in which eight people, the same number as Genesis, survived the Flood in a boat.[136]

A 17th century CE Jesuit missionary, in a very rare Latin volume of his *History of China*, wrote that before the Great Catastrophe occurred, *"Four seasons succeeded each other regularly and without confusion. There were no... excessive rains. The Sun and moon, without ever being clouded, furnished a light purer and brighter than now. The five planets kept on their course without any inequality. Nothing harmed man, nor did he harm anything... then the Second Heaven [Wilkins equates this to Second Sun in American traditions]... the pillars of heaven were broken. The earth shook to its foundations. The sky sank lower towards the north. The Sun, moon and stars changed their motions. The earth fell to pieces and the waters in its bosom uprushed with violence and overflowed... the Sun went into eclipse..."[137]*

Censorius, a Roman chronologist (3rd century CE), wrote that at the end of every Great Year of six Babylonian SARS our planet undergoes a complete revolution, *"...catastrophes attend the change, with great earthquakes and cosmical throes."[138]* By the time of Censorius, the NER chronology of 600-year periods was already lost and the meaning of "shar" was unknown. There has always been two meanings to this word that referred to a cycle, or revolution. The lesser idea was that of a turning of night into day, a single day. The other was a 120-year period, the Great Shar. Censorius' data was bad, but it preserved the same concept of a long period, like the 3000th year being the end of an age, finished by catastrophe.

Wilkins notes that the ancient Greeks believed that at the end of every 12,000 years the *beds of the oceans are displaced*, and a major deluge occurs. *"The priests of the sanctuaries kept in strict secrecy any notions of how long such a catastrophe might last, and all about its details."*[139] Just as with Plato's 9000 years actually being 9000 lunations for a sum of 690 years (five 138-year Phoenix visits), so too is the 12,000 years an exaggerated duration for 1200 years, from 3439 BCE to the Great Deluge in 2239 BCE, both years well-documented for major flood disasters.

Diodorus Siculus, drawing on the records of old Carthage inherited from Phoenicia, and relating histories of the ancients, tells of an old destruction story that Wilkins interpreted, stating, *"...some cosmic body... approached our own planet, the earth, after the Sun had vanished behind vast clouds into a night of blackness, and brought on an appalling cataclysm. The Great Deluge of the Old World myths and Genesis..."*[140]

There are over 200 known sunken ancient cities beneath the Mediterranean Sea.[141] The majority of these cities are unknown, which easily provides us a general date for their drowning. The locations of many of them reveals that the Mediterranean Sea was once no sea at all, and this was within the Old Bronze Age period. The Mediterranean Sea has been basically the same from the earliest times from which tradition and letters were passed down in the region, however, to have sunken unknown cities that were not of those civilizations during the Middle and Late Bronze Ages reveals that they were all part of an earlier civilization that occupied low-lying valleys and plains. Only later were they drowned in a single devastating flood, which reveals that the deluge waters *never left*. This particular flood was the creation of a whole *new sea*.

A very extensive Caucasian civilization inhabited the coasts of Europe, Britain, Ireland, Scotland, and northern Europe to Spain and France – and a second Caucasian culture dwelled in multitudes of cities in the interior land of great lakes that were separating Europe, Asia, and Africa. The Atlantic flood drowned many of the valley-dwelling

Caucasians with only their interior settlements surviving along the newly created coasts of the newly forged Mediterranean Sea. This new water gateway was soon filled with those Caucasian groups that were occupying the isles and coasts of Europe.

A British Archaeology (1997) article, *Comets and Disasters in the Bronze Age*, reads, *"At some time around 2300 BCE, give or take a century... a large number of the major civilizations of this world collapsed simultaneously, it seems. The Akkadian Empire in Mesopotamia, the Old Kingdom of Egypt, the Early Bronze Age civilization in Israel, Anatolia, and Greece, as well as the Indus Valley civilization in India, the Hilmand civilization of Afghanistan, and the Hongshan culture of China – the first urban civilizations in the world – all fell into ruin at more or less the same time."*[142] This article lists abrupt climate changes, sudden sea level changes, catastrophic inundations, widespread seismic activity and evidence for massive volcanic activity.[143] G. Ernest Wright wrote that the early Bronze Age destruction was so violent *"...that scarcely a vestige survived."*[144]

Malta is strong proof for a Mediterranean Valley Civilization in prehistory, Old Bronze Age.[145]

The floor of Malta temples were covered in about three feet of silt.[146]

Ancient temples have been found at Malta, Hagar Qim, Mnajdra and Ggantija, some with colossal stones 20 feet high.[147]

Earthquakes were experienced at the time of the Mediterranean flooding. During the quakes the land bridge between Europe and Africa broke, now called the Pillars of Hercules, or Strait of Gibraltar. The Atlantic Ocean poured into the breach, flooding the fertile valleys of Middle Earth (Mediterranean). The homeland of the Caucasian race was drowned as the Atlantic tore apart the land bridge to fill up the vast tract of valleys now submerged beneath the Mediterranean Sea, the Tyrrhenian Sea, the Adriatic Sea, and the Aegean Sea. The floodwaters, at over a hundred feet high and moving over three hundred miles an hour, broke through the Bosphorus and raised the Black Sea.[148]

On Malta, Ellul wrote, *"All this destruction caused by the colossal wave rushing from west to east can be witnessed in the stone age megalithic ruins of Hagar Qim. When one examines these ruins closely, one will easily see that the wall facing directly westwards has been completely destroyed. This wall which had to bear the brunt of this gigantic wave, followed by a rush of water in its wake, could not withstand the onslaught... huge blocks of stone from the western wall have been blown off from their original position and piled up in a heap... "*[149]

In the Legend of Cadiz in Spain, the Pillars of Hercules had split open and the Mediterranean world was flooded.[150]

Cadiz in Spain was built after the Mediterranean flooded.

At this time, massive earthquakes destroyed Puma Punku in Bolivia, South America. It was constructed of sandstone and andesite blocks up to 27 feet long and weighed 300 tons. The structure was destroyed in an earthquake of epic proportions. The Puma Punku construction was long before Tiahuanacu. At this time, Tiahuanacu was not built but later had more inferior building techniques than Puma Punku. Puma Punka had its clamps and geometric designs precisely cut into the andesite.[151]

When Puma Punku was constructed it was not high in the Andes Mountains like today. Those mountains were created by cataclysm – the whole South American continental plate was elevated thousands of feet during the geologic upheaval that later occured in 1687 BCE. The massive blocks of Puma Punku are scattered about like children's blocks, but nearby Tiahuanacu's are not.[152] Puma Punku is not only older than Tiahuanacu, but its building methods were technolithic, dating it from 3439-2647 BCE during the Contact Period. Christopher Dunn, British engineer, has found surfaces on stone at Puma Punku to be 5/1000th of an inch accurate; meaning that the flatness of the surface deviates only that little bit from being perfect.[153] Tiahuanacu on the other hand is not technolithic, not even post-technolithic (2647-2239 BCE), but entirely of the Heliolithic Period (2239-1687 BCE). Puma Punku was a Homo Anunna site laid waste at the Great Deluge when the *"foundations of the earth shook,"* and the site was held in such high regard that Tiahuanacu was built near its ruins shortly afterward.

In canons of the Chinese Emperor Yao (*The Book of Documents*, main canon Part One, the *Canon of Yao*, said to have been compiled by Confucius [551-479 BC] from much earlier sources), we read, *"In the life time of Yao, the Sun did not set for ten full days and the entire land was flooded."*[154]

The Flood story of Deucalion (son of Prometheus) and his wife Pyrrha is very prominent in Thessaly.[155]

To the Greeks, Noah was not remembered as distant from them, but fondly, as Nereus, with his daughters being the Nereids, a memory of their *origin from the sea.*

The *Epic of Gilgamesh* on the Great Deluge states, *"When the seventh day came, the cyclone ceased."*[156]

Egerton Sykes wrote, *"It cannot be too strongly emphasized that while there have been several world disasters, there appears to have been only one quasi-universal deluge within the limits of the historic period."*[157]

Lucian relates that the Aramaean (Syrian) flood tradition is of Deucalion.[158] Thus the Greeks inherited the Amorite Flood tradition.

In the Welsh Triads, we find that in the history of Prydain (Briton) there were three great catastrophes. The first was the eruption of the Lake of Waves, or Great Flood, when all humans died, save a man and a woman on a raft.[159] Welsh Triads date back to the 13th century CE, but are connected to very ancient traditions.[160]

The Phoenix approach caused earth's core to heat up at the time of the Great Flood. In addition to the collapse of the vapor canopy, subsurface heat and pressure increased through earth's mantle, pushing subterranean water reservoirs in the crust to the surface. Much of the floodwaters that drowned men were also from a violently heated water table that boiled out onto the surface. A superheated crust evaporated the water and deposits were baked into the strata according to weight and density, even while rains from above continued. After the collapse of the thick vapor canopy, the new atmospheric moisture canopy from the heated crust was contaminated with volcanic ash, which then rapidly cooled the planet. The entire fossil record we have is evidence of a planet that has been flooded and cooked at least three times.

Lenormant wrote, *"While the tradition of the deluge holds so considerable a place in the legendary memories of all branches of the Aryan race, the monuments and original texts of Egypt, with their many cosmogonic speculations, have not afforded one, event distant, allusion to this cataclysm."*[161]

The Great Flood destroyed the Caucasian homelands, but the urban centers of the red and yellow races continued.

During this event, the Atlantic Ocean burst through the Strait of Gibraltar, filling the tree-filled valleys of Middle Earth (Mediterranean), previously a paradise of freshwater lakes, rivers and forests. The sudden incursion of 100-foot high walls of foaming seawater drowned over 200 cities and the floods, like fingers, raced through the lowlands, cutting off the escape of untold myriads of communities. Only birds crowding the skies in the west gave any warning that death was approaching. By this time, people heard the distant roaring of the raging deluge as it moved hundreds of miles per hour, and it was too late to escape. Whole occupied lands were submerged. Sardinia and Corsica, with Sicily, were separated from the Italian-Tunisian land bridge that vanished under the new surf, totally isolating Malta.

The Atlantic seawater walls spread over northern Africa as quakes caused a subsidence that sank the Giza Complex pyramids below the surface of the newly formed Mediterranean. The quake that broke the Gibraltar wide open may be the same as that which lowered the Delta region of northern Egypt. The walls of water pushed northward through the Aegean, creating thousands of islands. The force of the world's entire sea-level pushed the Atlantic onward, to penetrate the Dardanelles and create the Sea of Marmara, before busting through the Bosporus land-bridge with violence, to fill the freshwater Pontus Lake in the creation of the Black Sea. This is where William Ryan, Walter Pitman, and Ian Wilson's research enlightens us, while also committing chronological blasphemy. These men put forth the theory of the Black Sea Flood being that of Noah's Flood, though they are all unaware that the Atlantic's flooding to create the Mediterranean and Aegean seas is what also created the Black Sea. Ironically, this event *was* Noah's Flood (2239 BCE), but their dating of 5600 BCE for the Black Sea Deluge and Noah's Flood (they claim) is actually an error of 3360 years. A concise review of their popular theory will demonstrate this dating error.

Ian Wilson in *Before the Flood* cites Diodorus Siculus concerning a reference to flooding in the Aegean that separated Samothrace from the mainland, leaving it an island when the Great Pontus Lake was over flooded.[162] Wilson notes that to Diodorus, the flooding of Samothrace in the Aegean and that of Pontus Lake were contemporaneous, separated only by the Dardanelles and Bosporus. Wilson, Ryan and Pitman are aware that the Mediterranean-Aegean broke through the Bosporus to flood the Black Sea, but are unaware that in 5600 BCE there were no saltwater Mediterranean or Aegean seas, only scattered freshwater lakes. Their model would push back the construction of the 200+ cities (now deep beneath the surface of today's Mediterranean) to a time *before* 5600 BCE and this is untenable. Wilson notes that,

- American Bob Karlin while aboard the research vessel *Knorr*, found evidence of a one-time, massive underwater sedimentary avalanche at the location where the Bosporus joins the Black Sea.[16]
- Scientific evidence shows a rapid transformation from a freshwater lake to a larger saltwater sea.[164]
- A drowned former coastline, an old shoreline, was discovered at a depth of 358 feet under the surface of the Black Sea by oceanographer Dr. Petko Dimitrov of Bulgaria.[165]
- At the bottom of the Black Sea bed is a 40-inch thick layer of sapropel, a mud thick with decomposed plant and animal remains from a prior freshwater lake.[166]

Their 5600 BCE date for Noah's Flood completely defies every interpretation of biblical, pseudopigraphical, ancient textual, and traditional deluge dating of the Chinese, Near Eastern and even old American accounts. 5600 BCE is 28 centuries prior to the well-established construction date of the Great Pyramid of Giza, which by testimony of multitudes of ancient sources, was built centuries before the Flood of Noah, a construction date equally supported by carbon dating. Ian Wilson supports this 5600 BCE date by the official-but-ridiculous date of Çatal Höyük, a site known to have 14 levels of occupation built one on top of the other, suggesting about a thousand years of settlement.[167] Çatal Höyük is not as old as publicized. It was buried after it was abandoned and in 1961-1965 CE, excavations at the site by Mellaart uncovered surprisingly good sanitation, a well-ordered refuse system, white plastered walls painted with abstract, textile-type designs,[168] landscape paintings,[169] the breeding and domestication of bovines,[170] use of wheat and barley to bake bread,[171] the crafting of baked clay statuettes, with one of a woman wearing a very brief miniskirt, and blouse with shoulder straps,[172] also basketry and exceptional wood crafting and pottery,[173] use of polished obsidian mirrors and boring holes through small beads, as well as the art of metallurgy.[174] At Çatal Höyük, carpeting on the floors was found to be of exceptional quality comparable to the finest woven today.[175] Everywhere else in the world these innovations did not appear until *after* 3439 BCE. Wilson's own use of Çatal Höyük's discoveries actually aids us in discarding the false antiquity of Çatal Höyük and of their own 5600 BCE date for the Great Deluge.

Ian Wilson shows how at Çatal Höyük the Great Mother Goddess was worshipped and the Bull Cult flourished.[176] Depictions of the Goddess show her giving birth while enthroned between two leopards.[177] The goddess-between-two-leopards motif was specifically a post-Diluvian symbol known widely throughout excavated Near East sites that date to about 2000 BCE, not 5600 BCE – an absurd dating, especially because Wilson also cites the 1968 CE discovery of archeologist Paul Lapp, who found at Taanach in northern Israel an 11th century BCE artifact depicting the goddess Astarte, frontally naked between two lions beside a young bull. Wilson notes the association to Çatal Höyük's Mother Goddess.[178] This leap of 4600 years passes through *35 centuries* for which we have archeological data and wherein are found no Great Mother Goddess-between-leopards artifacts. Wilson seems to recognize this major distance in time in his bibliographic note for Chapter 10 #4, writing, *"After the desertion [Çatal Höyük]... the sixth millennium BC there follows a long period for which the record remains a blank."*[179] The record has never been blank. Nothing has been found in confirmation of this cult's high antiquity reaching to 5600 BCE because the civilizations that revered the Great Mother Goddess did not even develop until after a widespread awakening, post-3439 BCE. Wilson further provides more evidence that Çatal Höyük nor the Black Sea Flood occurred so early. In *Before the Flood,* he notes the similarities between Çatal Höyük and the Minoan civilization of Crete. The Minoans were a cattle people who worshipped the Great Mother Goddess; they were adherents of the Bull Cult and prior to the discovery of Çatal Höyük, the Minoans were virtually the first known people to paint their walls with landscapes, and to plaster them.[180] Ironically, Wilson further notes that 4000 years separated his dating of Çatal Höyük and the height of Minoan culture.[181] Even the horned shrines of the Minoans were identical to those of Çatal Höyük.[182] And these are similar even to those horned facades found on Malta, where images of the same fat Great Mother Goddess were also found.[183] He also notes that the labyrinthine interior of the Hypogeum on Malta is very similar to the layout of Çatal Höyük.[184] The widespread Bronze Age motif of the double-ax, or labrys, has been found at both Çatal Höyük and Minoan Crete.[185] All of these examples and more infer that the two cultures were contemporary and that the Minoan chronology is correct, while the Çatal Höyük is pure fancy.

As the Minoan civilization dates to about 2500-1447 BCE and Malta was destroyed by the Mediterranean Flood in 2239 BCE, Wilson's own arguments contradict his 5600 BCE dating of both the Black Sea Flood and the antiquity of Çatal Höyük. NO HUMAN ARCHITECTURE has ever been found dating to the 4th, 5th or 6th millennium BCE. Not even Göbekli Tepe dates to the 5th millennium BCE. The fact that a settlement was buried in layers of mud is not evidence of high antiquity. Many European cities today not even eight centuries old have been rebuilt several times due to floods and quakes, often with newer infrastructures erected on top of the older levels.

Bull-sacrifice and bull-fighting has no American or Oriental counterpart, nor African or even northern European counterpart. In the ancient world, it was very distinctively Mediterranean-Minoan.

In Çatal Höyük, artwork found depicts a gigantic bird eating a man, with the bird being at least ten times larger than the human.[186] On the other side of the world in North America, at Arizona in the Petrified Forest, is a petroglyph of an enormous, long-billed water fowl holding a human in its beak.[187] When this petroglyph was made, Arizona was not the barren wasteland it is today and the trees of Petrified Forest were not stone at that time... this denotes that gigantic birds preyed on humans on both sides of the world in pre-cataclysm times.

This is the beginning of the Heliolithic Period, with intelligent civilizations that have left behind certain aspects of their cultures – things were preserved only in certain areas of the sciences, engineering, and old hardware innovations of Post-Technolithic culture in the quarrying, transportation, dressing, and emplacement of megalithic building materials; new methods of construction called cyclopean, in a widespread effort to reduce earthquake damage.

That dinosaurs were millions of years in age is in question due to the discovery of an anatomically correct brontosaurus image found patterned on a sword blade, found among Roman artifacts near Tucson, Arizona.[188]

Philo Judaeus in *On Rewards and Punishments IV,* [189] wrote that the Greek Deucalion and the biblical Noah were the same person.

In Samothrace the flood hero was Dardanus, when, according to Diodorus, the sea rose and covered a great part of the level country of the island, causing survivors to flee in to the mountains. [190] The Dardanelles were named after these Flood survivors, the very islands that were broken in the Mediterranean Flood that also created the Black Sea.

The Deucalion Flood so damaged the Hellenic coast opposite the islands of Rhodes and Cos that, *"...the fruits of the earth were rotted and spoiled for a long time together, famine prevailed, and through corruption of the air, plague and pestilence depopulated and laid the towns and cities waste,"* according to Diodorus (Book V). [191]

Sumerian records hold that the Great Deluge occurred during the reign of the seventh king, but Greek tradition holds that Deucalion's Flood happened in the seventh generation. [192]

The Deucalion account of Lucian tells how animals came to his ark, two-by-two. [193]

The north celestial pole moved from the stellar background of Draconis into Ursa Minor. Astronomers claim earth is precessing in space due to this. They offer a neatly packaged theory called precession. Claiming that gravitational (another hypothetical) interactions of the Sun, moon, and earth's equitorial bulge causes a wobble like a spinning top, one full rotation requiring 26,000 years. [194] Whether real or imagined, this wobble is not the cause of the change in pole stars, but an effect. Precession as a phenomenon is not the cause, but the continued effect of the cataclysmic pole shift caused by Phoenix. Our moon was not even in orbit around earth 26,000 years ago, but was moved into its present position in 4039 BCE, barely 6,600 years ago.

Alexander Thom noted that the megalithic builders, as inventors of these impressive monuments, belonged to a *pre-Mediterranean culture.* [195] This is scientific acknowledgement that a civilized people existed in the Mediterranean (Middle Earth) before the Mediterranean had become a salt water sea.

The Sumerians appear to have been constantly fearful of sudden and catastrophic upheavals, according to Stephen E. Flowers, Ph.D. [196]

2239 BCE is the date for the Great Flood in Ussher's chronology in *Annals of the World* (1658), but he was 110 years in error – assigning this date to 2349 BCE, a mistake he makes consistently in old world dates because his Year One was 4004 BCE, off by 109 years from 3895 BCE (1 AM).

James Ussher, Archbishop of Armaugh, completed his famous *Annals of the World: Deduced From the Origin of Time*, in 1654. He dated the Flood at the year 1656, and he likewise died in 1656 CE, the Annals being published two years after his death in 1658 CE.

People of Athens, Greece, had 120 days in the year set aside for festivals,[197] which is precisely a third of 360.

The Frisian *Oera Linde Book* reads that before the Great Flood cataclysm *"...the years were not counted."*[198]

Berossus in Babylonia wrote that from the crowning of the first king of the Ten King Dynasty to the Great Deluge, passed 432,000 years. From Aloros I to the Flood [199] being 1200 years (432,000▯360 *days* = 1200). *Atrahasis Epic* holds that the Anunnaki were upset every 1200 years due to human overpopulation.[200]

In the *Atrahasis Epic*, before the floodwaters appeared the sky darkened black.

Harold T. Wilkins in *Mysteries of Ancient South America* wrote, *"... some cosmic body... approached our own planet, the earth, after the Sun had vanished behind vast clouds into a night of blackness, and brought on an appalling cataclysm – the Great Deluge of the Old World."*[201]

In the Mayan Quiche *Popul Vuh* we read that, *"...at a terrific flood, the earth darkened, and it rained night and day. Thus was accomplished the ruin of the race of men which was given up to destruction."* Wilkins wrote that the disasters were caused by *"...the violent disturbance of the earth's orbit and the setting up of an appalling centrifugal force which drove our planet farther from the Sun."*[202]

Jesuit missionary Padre Martin Martinius, in his rare *History of China*, wrote of the Great Flood as known to the ancient Chinese, when the pillars of heaven were broken (pole shift), the sky sank lower towards the north; the Sun, moon, and stars altered their motions, the Sun went dark and water destroyed the earth.[203]

The Bacchic account of the Deluge claims that it was caused by **Typhon**.[204]

Rabbinical sources claim that before the Flood many arks were being built[205] and they were of incredible size.[206]

Wilkins described the sky at the time of the vapor canopy collapse, stating *"...it shone with a brilliant light reflected from the Sun, falling on a thick coating of ice – the glaciosphere. This split and fell on the earth, exposing a layer of red earth, which in turn, fell on the earth in a rain like blood."*[207]

Phoenix is named in a cryptic passage by Nostradamus concerning the end of a 670-year period. *"Many will die before the Phoenix dies, until 670 his dwelling shall endure..."* This 670 years concerns the 670 years of Anunnaki supremacy on earth before the Deluge, mentioned in the Sumerian King List. This time frame ran from 2909 BCE to the Flood in 2239 BCE.

Nostradamus further revealed an awareness of the Phoenix in his letter when he described that the Great Flood occurred after a 1242-year period, which is exactly 138x9, with the Phoenix appearing every 138 years.

The evil goddess was called Itzpapalotl by the Aztecs, she having a pair of obsidian (black) knives (instruments of sacrifice). She is associated with Venus. In the *Codex (Letellier)*, we find, *"...she caused death to the world, and is one of the six constellations that fell from the sky at the time of the Deluge."*[208]

Eudoxus of Cnidus, a brilliant contemporary of Plato (he was a mathematician, astronomer, lawmaker and doctor), wrote, *"...the Egyptians reckon a month as a year."*

Diodorus wrote that it was popular in antiquity to reckon the year by the lunar cycle.

The Vedic Hindu *Mahabharata* reads, "...on the seventh day after this, the three worlds shall sink beneath the ocean... thou shalt embark on a great ship."

A Sumerian fragment on the Deluge reads, "For seven days and seven nights the Flood swept over the land."

It is found in the *Bhagavata Purana*, *"In the course of seven days the ocean overflowed, and the earth was submerged in continual rain."*

The Aymara people of Peru (indigenous to Lake Titicaca) maintain that in the Great Deluge "...the Sun was hidden by a great darkness."
In the Aztec history of Ixtlilxóchitl, the Water Sun Age ends in cataclysm, the Earth Sun Age beginning.[209]
A common theme in antiquity was that at the Flood, the Sun had been born, implying that the prior one had died.
The Babylonian *Talmud*, called *Berakthoth*, conveys that the giants before the Flood had double-rows of teeth (hyperdontia).[210]
Wilkins in 1952 wrote, *"The old Jews in Babylon, and in old Egypt, took over and mixed up and garbled for purely nationalist reasons, stories about the Great Cataclysm derived from far more ancient races."*[211]
Antiquarian Harold T. Wilkins, in his 1947 CE work *Mysteries of Ancient South America*, documents parallels between the Great Flood and the later Ogygian Flood (1687 BCE) – similarities in the historical records so uncanny that he ventures to propose that they might be the same disaster. He is wrong, as they are 552 years apart, however, he is correct that they were caused by the exact same phenomenon – Phoenix. Wilkins wrote, *"When the Great Deluge of Noah and Ogyges happened... convulsions of the shuddering earth and sea stretched right around our globe from the Pacific across South America to the shores of Africa... right into the Mediterranean, till they shook the old Levant and a more ancient Greece. In the skies of terrible night shone a giant comet, or wandering star, or planet... but which brought such destruction on the earth that those who survived the disasters regained sanity only slowly...*[212] *The Sun appeared like a ball of blood."*[213]
The turtle, or tortoise, was anciently associated with the Great Flood.[214]
The Jewish authors of Genesis and the Old Testament altered a very important element of the ancient Flood story. In Genesis, it is Almighty God who destroyed the world in a Flood, but this was a 6th-5th century BCE monotheistic invention. All historical Flood records of Sumer and Babylonia of the early-to-later 2nd millennium BCE relate that the Anunnaki gods tried to exterminate mankind.[215]
In all his acts, the god Enki was against the ruling Anunnaki, ever in favor of humanity.
The main Anunnaki gods are known as The Seven, though only six are ever named.[216] In connection to them, *"...perhaps forming the unknown seventh of the group, is the Sedu. But little is known of him."*[217] This

deity, Sedu, is the origin of the biblical deity named El Shaddai, later said in the Bible to have the title of Yahweh, or Jehovah. The Sumerian ideogram for Sedu was ALAD.[218]

In the 6th-5th centuries BCE, the Jewish scholars exiled in Babylonia learned two very widely-known things about the Ancient World, found in the old libraries there. They discovered in text after text that the Pre-Flood World was exactly 1656 years in duration and that during this period there was a magnificently powerful, ten-king dynasty that ended at the Deluge. The Jews took these two ancient known facts and wrote the fictionalized account of Ten Patriarchs, whose total lifespans in the Genesis genealogy, when added together, add up to 1656 years. Genesis becomes the first document in history to claim that men lived lifespans of three to over nine centuries. Such longevity in old records is reserved only to the Anunnaki *"gods"* and their progeny – like Gilgamesh/Nimrod and other Nephilim. No other texts antedating the 6th century BCE claim any unusual longevity for ordinary mortals. Noah is no exception. Many traditions mention a flood survivor and ark builder – however, none attribute to him any unusual long life. Pure Jewish fiction.

Two genealogies in Genesis – a Ten Patriarchs line beginning with Adam, and the Eight Patriarchs beginning with Cain – are mere Jewish inventions modelled after the Babylonian documented histories of a Ten-King Dynasty and an Eight-King Dynasty, both found mentioned in Sumerian tablets and prisms.

Hipparchus published a catalogue of 1080 fixed stars.[219]

Rashi's statement that *"...every 1656 years a similar disaster occurs,"* identifies 3895 BCE (Year One) as having a cataclysm similar to the Great Flood, as well as 583 BCE, which appears to have had a night time disaster in the Americas and Far East.

DAYS, not years, were calculated in the time of the antediluvian world. In the *Epic of Gilgamesh* we read, *"As for mankind, numbered are his days."*[220]

The *Popul Vuh* reports on the cataclysm, *"Then the waters were agitated by the will of the Heart of Heaven, and a great inundation came upon the heads of these creatures... they were engulfed, and a resinous thickness descended from heaven... the face of the earth was obscured..."*[221]

A heart is always red, so the "HEART of Heaven" is RED, like the Phoenix. "Resinous thickness" with the Phoenix is also a common theme reported throughout history.

Chronologist Alex Gleason in 1890 CE wrote that the Flood occurred in the 1656th year.[222]

In Babylonia the Seven Kings are often blamed for the Great Flood, but the older Akkadian and Sumerian versions have Eight Kings – beginning with an Alu-lim, a title scholars note derives from a feminine root. Having Eight Kings is the origin of the Scorpion King motif, an arachnid, and of the Spider Grandmother, the Goddess before the Flood, who ruled BEFORE kingship was established. So we find here a transfer of gender for the ruling deities.

The flood catastrophe that ruined the world of Bochica occurred at the same time Bochica instructed his descendants and the survivors to adopt a SUN calendar. The people blamed the Moon for the flood destruction, claiming she to be a goddess (Viracocha and Thunupa). Viracocha is widely considered male, but some traditions have given him a dual nature. And a story of Thunupa tells of an older man who drifts from Lake Titicaca onto a *river*, and transforms the landscape as he goes – with a different Andean version being female, so both deities had dual natures. This tradition is the memory of the collapse of the vapor canopy, the pre-flood lunar calendar system of the dominant matriarchal goddess society that was ended abruptly by the flood disaster and the sudden appearance of the SUN, when the canopy fell. The patriarchal Sun societies overcame the female-dominant ruling dynasties.

The Greek writer Hyginus relates that one of the seven stars of the Pleiades named Elektra was so distraught at seeing the demise of her descendant, King Dardanus, during the fall of Troy, that she quit shining and fled as a *"hair star."* [comet].[223]

A vast civilized Caucasian civilization of city and town dwellers thrived in North America in the present regions of the United States. This civilization was destroyed and buried rapidly, and the North American plate was underwater for a very short period of time. The North American landmass was resurfaced, and the former surface is buried under today's United States. The archeological proofs offer convincing evidence of a pre-Flood North American civilization.

Though most of the megafauna perished in this event, some remnants survived.

This was the beginning of <u>Mound Builder</u> civilization.

The Hopi Indians claim that to survive the destruction of the First World the people had to descend into the underworld and live among the Ant People. While below, the world above was destroyed by fire and volcanoes. They emerged into the Second World. Shortly afterward, the Second World was ruined when it "turned over" twice and disrupted the heavens. But the ancestors of the Hopi survived again with the Ant People of the underworld. In the First World there was peace among the animals. In the Second World the Hopi learned village life, basketry and homemaking. Now in the Third World, the people multiplied after coming up to a red world (Phoenix fallout?) and they built mighty cities and kingdoms. The Third World was destroyed by Spider Grandmother with a Flood.[224]

1. Catastrophobia p. 169; 2. Augustine, City of God p. 15; 3. Pindar O.L.IX. 37; 4. Metamorphosis I. p. 240; 5. Lucian, De Dea Syra; 6. Appolodorus Lib. I; 7. The Great Pyramid: Its Divine Message p. 173; 8. Jasher 6:11; 9. Enoch 64:1-4; 10. History in Quotations p. 1; 11. History of the Christian Religion to the Year 200 p. 189; 12. Book of Jasher 6:13-25; 13. Chronology of Genesis p. 1; 14. The Natural Genesis vol. II p. 241; 15. Survivors of Atlantis p. 63; 16. Survivors of Atlantis p. 60; 17. Survivors of Atlantis p. 60; 18. Atlantis and the Kingdom of the Neanderthals p. 89; 19. The Incredible Discovery of Noah's Ark p. 57; 20. Baruch 3:26-28; 21. Atlantis: The Antediluvian World p. 64; 22. Genesis 7:11, 8:3-4; 23. Ramayana p. 109; 24. There were Giants Upon the Earth p. 27; 25. Underworld p. 27; 26. The Mahabharata, cited in Underworld, p. 135; 27. Uriel's Machine p. 132; 28. Ibid p. 122; 29. Atlantis Beneath the Ice p. 52; 30. The Lost Cities of Ancient Lemuria and the Pacific p. 93; 31. Atlantis: The Antediluvian World p. 67; 32. Atlantis: the Antediluvian World p. 78; 33. Ibid p. 80; 34. Atlantis: the Antediluvian World p. 81; 35. Ibid p. 81; 36. Ibid p. 81; 37. Ibid p. 81; 38. The 12ᵗʰ Planet p. 62; 39. Ibid p. 62; 40. The 12ᵗʰ Planet p. 400; 41. Ibid p. 400; 42. The 12ᵗʰ Planet p. 401; 43. Ibid p. 403; 44. The 12ᵗʰ Planet p. 405-406; 45. Ibid p. 406; 46. The 12ᵗʰ Planet p. 409; 47. Mysteries of the Ancient World p. 97; 48. Ibid p. 72; 49. The Epic of Gilgamesh and Old Testament Parallels p. 236; 50. When Time Began p. 20; 51. The Cosmic Code p. 95; 52. Ibid p. 98; 53. Ibid p. 107; 54. Ibid p. 110; 55. Monuments of the Incas p. 37; 56. Ibid p. 37; 57. Pyramids of the New World p. 116; 58. The Lost Realms p. 213; 59. The Wars of Gods and Men p. 35; 60. The Cradle of Civilization p. 104; 61. The Tigris Expedition p. 23; 62. Ibid p. 23; 63. Ibid p. 23; 64. Ibid p. 24; 65. The Tigris Expedition p. 327; 66. The Giza Prophecy p. 51, 57; 67. The Giza Prophecy p. 243-245; 68. The Gilgamesh Epic and Old Testament Parallels p. 239; 69. Atlantis: The Antediluvian World p. 74; 70. Atlantis: The Antediluvian World p. 75; 71. Atlantis: The Antediluvian World p. 76; 72. Earth Under Fire p. 235; 73. ibid p. 183; 74. Earth Under Fire p. 260-261; 75. Earth Under Fire p. 287; 76. Earth Under Fire p. 287; 77. From the Ashes of Angels p. 240; 78. Lost

Worlds of Ancient America p. 110; 79. The Origin of Biblical Traditions p. 149; 80. From the Ashes of Angels p. 340-342; 81. The Origin of Biblical Traditions p. 156; 82. Origin of Biblical Traditions p. 176; 83. Our Occulted History p. 152; 84. Atlantis in America p. 111; 85. Atlantis in America p. 175; 86. Atlantis in America p. 170; 87. The Sirius Mystery p. 280-281; 88. Ponder on This p. 62.; 89. Atlantis: The Antediluvian World p. 54; 90. Atlantis: The Antediluvian World p. 54; 91. ibid p. 54; 92. Atlantis: The Antediluvian World p. 59; 93. Atlantis: The Antediluvian World p. 83; 94. Atlantis: The Antediluvian World p. 84; 95. Atlantis: The Antediluvian World p. 208; 96. Atlantis: The Antediluvian World p. 209; 97. Atlantis: The Antediluvian World p. 175; 98. Surah XI.38. The Words of an Angel; 99. Atlantis: The Antediluvian World p. 179; 100. Atlantis: The Antediluvian World p. 103; 101. Atlantis: The Antediluvian World p. 96; 102. Atlantis: The Antediluvian World p. 324; 103. The History of Atlantis: Spence p. 149; 104. The History of Atlantis: Spence p. 149; 105. Our Sun-God: Christianity Before Christ p. 26; 106. Our Sun-God: Christianity Before Christ p. 33-34; 107. Ibid p. 36; 108. The Popul Vuh: Spence p. 100–101; 109. ibid p. 101; 110. Old Civilizations of Inca Land p. 86-87; 111. Zoroastrianism p. 87; 112. ibid. p. 88; 113. Zoroastrianism p. 89; 114. Atrahasis p. 18; 115. ibid p. 24; 116. Atlantis in America p. 68; 117. cited in Atlantis in America p. 69-70; 118. Atlantis in America p. 70; 119. Atlantis in America p. 70; 120. Atlantis in America p. 70; 121. Atlantis in America. Lewis Spence, p. 71; 122. Atlantis in America p. 71; 123. Atlantis in America p. 71-72; 124. Atlantis in America p. 72; 125. Atlantis in America p. 79; 126. Atlantis in America p. 79; 127. The Problem of Atlantis p. 214; 128. Flying Serpents and Dragons p. 94; 129. Flying Serpents and Dragons p. 101; 130. Mysteries of Ancient South America p. 12-13; 131. Mysteries of Ancient South America p. 13-14; 132. Mysteries of Ancient South America p. 15; 133. Mysteries of Ancient South America p. 115; 134. Mysteries of Ancient South America p. 16; 135. Mysteries of Ancient South America p. 16; 136. The Genesis Race p. 93; 137. Mysteries of Ancient South America p. 31, citing Hist. Sin..Lib. I p. 12; 138. Mysteries of Ancient South America p. 32; 139. Mysteries of Ancient South America p. 32; 140. Mysteries of Ancient South America p.87; 141. Lost Cities of Atlantis, Ancient Europe…, p. 103; 142. The Genesis Race p. 211-212; 143. ibid p. 214; 144. ibid. p. 212; 145. Lost Cities of Atlantis, Ancient Europe…, p. 191; 146. Lost Cities of Atlantis, Ancient Europe…, p. 198; 147. Lost Cities of Atlantis, Ancient Europe…, p. 190; 148. Lost Cities of Atlantis, Ancient Europe…, p. 178–179; 149. Lost Cities of Atlantis, Ancient Europe…, p. 206; 150. Lost Cities of Atlantis, Ancient Europe… p. 265; 151. Lost Cities and Ancient Mysteries of South America p. 138; 152. Lost Cities and Ancient Mysteries of South America p. 139; 153. Crimson Horizon: Rapa Nui: Navel of the World; 154. Lost Cities of Ancient Lemuria and the Pacific p. 93; 155. Atlantis: The Antediluvian World p. 76-77; 156. Atlantis: The Antediluvian World p. 64; 157. Atlantis: The Antediluvian World p. 69; 158. Atlantis: The Antediluvian World p. 70; 159. Atlantis: The Antediluvian World p. 79; 160. Atlantis: The Antediluvian World p. 79; 161. Atlantis: The Antediluvian World p. 80; 162. Before the Flood p. 155-157; 163. Before the Flood p. 45; 164. Before the Flood p. 44, 51; 165. Before the Flood p. 45-47; 166. Before the Flood p. 44; 167. Before the Flood p. 109; 168. Before the Flood p. 111; 169. Ibid. p. 112; 170. Ibid. p. 114; 171. Ibid. p. 115; 172. Ibid. p. 115; 173. Ibid. p. 117; 174. Ibid. p. 118; 175. Elder Gods in Antiquity p. 176; 176. Before the Flood p. 120; 177. Before the Flood p. 123; 178. Before the Flood p. 254; 179. Before the Flood p. 290; 180. Before the Flood p. 145; 181. Before the Flood p. 146; 182. Before the Flood p. 146; 183. Before the Flood p. 148; 184. Ibid. p. 148; 185. Elder Gods in Antiquity p. 176; 186. Lost Cities of North and Central America p. 329; 187. Lost Cities of North and Central America p. 329; 188. Lost Cities of North and Central America p. 331; 189. The Works of Philo p. 705; 190. The History of Atlantis: Spence p. 148-149; 191. The History of

Atlantis: Spence p. 29; 192. The History of Atlantis: Spence p. 29; 193. Before the Flood p. 260; 194. The Cosmic Connection p. 88; 195. In Search of Ancient Astronomies p. 89; 196. Lords of the Left-Hand Path p. 85; 197. Egypt, Greece and Rome p. 195; 198. Secret Cities of Old South America p. 367; 199. Secret Cities of Old South America p. 146; 200. Secret Cities of Old South America p. 163; 201. Ibid. p. 87; 202. Mysteries of Ancient South America p. 15-16; 203. Mysteries of Ancient South America p. 30-31; 204. Secret Cities of Old South America p. 432; 205. Space Travelers and the Genesis of the Human Form p. 183; 206. Secret Cities of Old South America p. 405; 207. Mysteries of Ancient South America p. 32; 208. Secret Cities of Old South America p. 55; 209. Secret Cities of Old South America p. 47; 210. Discovering Ancient Giants. p. 15; 211. Secret Cities of Old South America p. 405; 212. Mysteries of Ancient South America p. 10; 213. Mysteries of Ancient South America p. 13; 214. Secret Cities of Old South America p. 281; 215. The Gods of Eden, Bramly p. 46; 216. Doctrine of Sin in the Babylonian Religion p. 10-12; 217. Ibid. p. 13; 218. Doctrine of Sin in Babylonian Religion p. 25; 219. Symbols, Sex and the Stars p. 95; 220. Our Occult History p. 148; 221. Atlantis: The Andes Solution: p. 55; 222. Is The Bible From Heaven? p. 112; 223. The Greek Myths: Robert Graves, p. 154, sec. 41.6; 224. Book of the Hopi: Frank Waters p. 9-19.

www.ingramcontent.com/pod-product-compliance
Lightning Source LLC
Chambersburg PA
CBHW050012090426
42733CB00018B/2644